THE
PITTSBURGH STEELERS FANS'
BUCKET LIST

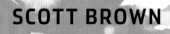

SCOTT BROWN

TRIUMPH
BOOKS

This book is available in quantity at special discounts for your group or organization. For further information, contact:

Triumph Books LLC
814 North Franklin Street
Chicago, Illinois 60610
(312) 337-0747
www.triumphbooks.com

Printed in U.S.A.
ISBN: 978-1-62937-254-9
Design by Andy Hansen
Page production by Patricia Frey
Photos courtesy of AP Images unless otherwise noted

To the memory of two of the biggest Steelers fans I knew: Lucas Murphy and Jack Lillie. Lucas didn't just live life; he attacked it. He went all out in everything he did and that included rooting for his beloved Steelers. Jack was the father of Jayson Lillie, who, like Lucas, I consider a brother, and man did he love his Steelers. I'm pretty sure his nickname of "Crazy Jack" has its roots in his allegiance to the Steelers. Those shots of rabid Steelers fans in games shown on NFL Films? Jack is in a couple of them and he was truly one of a kind. He and Lucas are still dearly missed by their loved ones.

Contents

Foreword

When I got drafted by the Steelers in 1988, the mystique of the organization jumped out to me. You had the legendary Rooney family and Chuck Noll. It was an honor for me to be a part of that and I got to meet Mr. Art Rooney before he passed away. Just to be a part of the 1990s teams that were going to the playoffs every year and playing in Super Bowl XXX, even though we lost, is something I will never forget.

People always ask me why Pittsburgh has such a great history with centers. I have no clue why that is and why center is such a prominent position in Pittsburgh. I do know that the tradition of excellence at the position motivated me when I moved to center after starting at guard my rookie season. I followed a legend in Mike Webster, who was a big influence on my career, and it's amazing to have joined him in the Pro Football Hall of Fame.

A common thing I hear from some of the guys who have been inducted is that you don't feel deserving and you still can't believe you were selected to the Pro Football Hall of Fame. It's phenomenal to be enshrined forever in Canton, Ohio, but it's something you just can't wrap your mind around. You reflect back on your career, and that's validation being enshrined in the Hall of Fame, but it's also kind of strange, the whole experience of being enshrined.

I'm just as proud, as far as my legacy, of having played for one team my entire career. I could have gone somewhere else in Plan B free agency and chased a few more dollars. But when guys do that they usually don't have as much success and I didn't want to go to another team. I was situated in Pittsburgh, loved the coaching staff, loved the ownership, and loved the fans. I had plenty of success in Pittsburgh and I wanted to be a one-team player. Now, you don't have the same player recognition when you look at the number of guys that move around. And I get why people do that and the financial reasons behind it. But for me it was important to stay with one team, and everyone associates me with the Steelers because that's the only team I ever played for. That is special.

I live in San Diego now and everywhere I go I see Steelers fans. People that know I played for Pittsburgh, of course they let me know they're Steelers fans. Or if I have a Pittsburgh hat on or a shirt and I'm walking they'll say, "Are you a Pittsburgh fan?" I'll say, "Oh, yeah," because most people don't know me out here. I do a lot of charity stuff with Marshall Faulk's foundation and Junior Seau's foundation but it's kind of incognito, and that's really the only time people know that I'm an athlete.

Anonymity is great. Living in Lexington, Kentucky, before I moved here, they called me the mayor of Lexington because I'm a hometown guy who played at University of Kentucky. I served on the Board of Trustees and on the athletic board for the University. No matter where I went it seemed like someone was always yelling my name. Sometimes it's nice just to be able to walk to the store unshaven and people don't care what you look like. I just love it. I never let people know that I'm a former NFL player unless they ask. Even then I won't give them a lot of information. I'm still the same low-key guy I was when I played at Kentucky and then for the Steelers.

There are no shortage of items for Steelers fans when it comes to a bucket list. There is one obvious one that jumps to mind: if a Steelers fan has never been to Canton, Ohio, and visited the Pro Football Hall of Fame, they have to do it. It's a phenomenal facility and they are doing new renovations right now. There is a lot of football history and it's a great place. It's close to Pittsburgh, within driving distance, so there's no excuse not to visit if you're a Steelers fan.

Being a Pittsburgh Steeler to me meant being proud and striving for excellence every day. Continuing to uphold the winning tradition and add to the rich history of a storied franchise is something I took very seriously. I hope I did my part.

—Dermontti Dawson
May 2016

Dermontti Dawson played all 13 of his NFL seasons for the Steelers, made seven consecutive Pro Bowls, and was a first-team All-Pro selection while defining excellence at center—and redefining the position. Dawson, a member of the NFL's All-Decade team in the 2000s, received football's ultimate honor in 2012, when he was elected to the Pro Football Hall of Fame. His No. 63 is among a handful of jersey numbers that have not been officially retired by the Steelers but have not been issued since he retired.

Introduction

The bits and pieces I remember of the first house where I grew up outside of Pittsburgh are like a jigsaw puzzle that has been scattered by a blast of wind or an overeager puppy. They are all over the place and it would take time to piece them together and form a clear picture.

One memory, however, stands out nearly four decades later, and I can still see my dad trying to sneak an extra french fry or two from my dinner plate by pointing to a screen door and saying "there's Mean Joe Greene," or "there's Franco Harris."

My head snapped around every damn time. Though in my defense, if I believed a plump, bearded man with a sack of presents jumped down my chimney every Christmas, was one of my Steelers heroes showing up on my back porch really so implausible?

My mom knew how to use the Steelers against me too.

I fought piano lessons at every turn as a grade-schooler, a battle I had no chance of winning. What really checkmated me and any feeble argument I could make: my mom countering that if Lynn Swann took ballet I could embrace the finer arts too.

I suspect such childhood memories, which include a neighborhood dog named Lambert and even an eponymous rodent named Jack Hamster, make me like a lot of other kids who grew up in Western Pennsylvania in the 1970s.

The Steelers were rock stars before we knew what rock stars were, higher powers deserving of our adulation and worship.

To us there was no "same old Steelers," a refrain that accompanied the losses that came too frequently before Neil Armstrong walked on the moon—and even for a period after Chuck Noll and Greene joined the organization in 1969. We were the first generation of Steelers fans weaned on winning.

They won big too, and with a colorful cast of characters that enhanced the Steelers' appeal, and they did so at a time when Pittsburgh needed it most. The Steelers' rise came as the steel industry collapsed and their four Super Bowl championships from 1974 to '79 provided a reason to cheer and to puff out chests in an economically depressed region that also battled the outside image of a rust-belt city on the decline.

The Steelers' success turned an ordinary dish rag into a towel-waving clarion call and made it impossible to label them as just a Sunday phenomenon in Pittsburgh. What young boy did not dress up as his favorite Steelers player for Halloween? Who didn't know of a pet named after the Steelers? Who else had to take piano lessons because Swann made acrobatic catches—in the Super Bowl, no less—look routine?

The Steelers, alas, could not hover forever at the impossibly high bar they set in the '70s, and like every other dynasty in the history of mankind theirs crashed under the weight of their own success.

The insidious encroachment of age eventually reeled in the great players from the '70s, and seemingly one by one, too. The drafts that turned the Steelers into a dynasty—and started a pipeline to the Pro Football Hall of Fame—weren't nearly as good after they started winning Super Bowls.

And they certainly weren't good enough to hold off gravity.

It took the Steelers more than a decade to return to the Super Bowl after winning their fourth one. Another 10 years passed after losing to the Cowboys in Super Bowl XXX before the Steelers finally broke through and captured the elusive one for the thumb.

Steelers fandom has been passed down in my younger sister's family. Here, my nieces pose at their home in suburban Minneapolis before the Steelers' playoff win over the Bengals on January 9, 2016.

I never did hear from Lambert but can't help but think, *Damn, he's still got it as an intimidator.*

Harrison, too, will probably never lose that.

His story is one of the great ones in Steelers history and there is more on that later in the book. One personal experience in particular with Harrison would have left me a little weak in the knees had I actually been front and center for it.

It happened in 2008 while Harrison was in the midst of a monster season that would earn him NFL Defensive Player of the Year honors. The Steelers had beaten the Jaguars in Jacksonville in early October and I hung around the locker room that night later than most of the media along with longtime Steelers beat writer Mark Kaboly.

Harrison had seemingly been held on every other pass play, and he was still seething about it when we approached him. When we asked him why there weren't more holding penalties called against the Jaguars he said that the referees must have "had money" on the game.

It was clearly Harrison's anger and frustration talking and I believe I portrayed it as such in the story that followed. But the NFL is sensitive to anything related to gambling and NFL commissioner Roger Goodell hammered Harrison with a fine.

The NFL also wrote to Harrison that he had been fined because of something *I* wrote and he taped the letter on the wall next to his locker. During a media scrum after he had received the fine, Harrison said, "Which one of you is Scott Brown? That mother[bleep] owes me $25,000."

I am not positive that was his exact quote because I happened to be at the other end of the locker room at the time. That is close to what he said because the reporters who heard him were more than happy to relay it to me with a laugh—and warning that James Harrison was looking for me.

I never heard a word about it from Harrison, much to my relief, and he probably still doesn't know who I am. I thought about taking $25,000 in Monopoly money to Harrison but then figured that if I didn't catch him in the right mood the joke could quickly go awry. And I didn't really want to think about what Harrison, as ornery as any player I've ever covered, might do with those Monopoly bills if he wasn't in the best of moods.

* * *

I approached this book from the perspective of a sportswriter who covered the Steelers for almost a decade more than as someone who grew up rooting for them. That is because most of the Steelers games I have attended have been in a working capacity, not as a fan.

But I also realized that tackling this project strictly through the prism of an impassionate observer would be a disservice to readers. I grew up in Western Pennsylvania. I know how passionate fans are about the Steelers and what the Steelers mean to Pittsburgh.

That is why the scores of interviews I conducted include former players and others connected with the organization but also fans and peripheral figures who make the Steelers unique.

The first three chapters in particular break down items on the Steelers fans' bucket list. Here is a baseline guide as far as cost is concerned:

Free

$= $1–$9 per person

$$ = $10–$99 per person

$$$ = $100–$999 per person

$$$$ = $1,000–$9,999 per person

$$$$$ = $10,000+ per person

The only thing that exceeds $10,000 is on my Steelers bucket list: going to a Super Bowl and paying top dollar for everything from accommodations and entertainment to transportation and game-day tickets.

There is also a scale for difficulty and the colors of a traffic light are used here. A ⬤ light means it's easy to accomplish, such as going to a training-camp practice. A ⬤ light indicates that it might take some work. A ⬤ light means to stop and think before deciding to do something.

The items throughout the book are accompanied by one to five bucket symbols, relative to where they rank on a bucket list, with five the highest. Everything included in this book is worthy of a Steelers bucket list; some just rank higher than others in my opinion.

I talked to so many interesting people for this book and gained an even greater appreciation for why Black and Gold fans proudly consider themselves a part of Steelers Nation. I hope you enjoy reading it as much as I did reporting and writing it.

I also hope the book becomes your guide as you start checking off items on your Steelers bucket list.

that. The best way for teams to navigate that delicate balance is to make Sundays (or Mondays or Thursdays) an experience and not just a game, and few, if any, cities do this better than Pittsburgh.

The North Side generates a certain electricity when the Steelers are at home and it starts pulsating long before kickoff. A massive Black and Gold party rages for hours before moving inside to Heinz Field. There fans wave Terrible Towels, lose what is left of their voices, and cheer a team that is a civic institution.

Pittsburghers love their football and they especially love their Steelers. TV can't completely capture this passion and this buzz, as much convenience as it provides. That is why attending a game at Heinz Field and turning it into an experience has to be at the top of a Steelers fan's bucket list.

· ·

Get an Early Start

Tailgating can be found in all forms around Heinz Field. An open stretch underneath the winding concrete of a parking garage near the stadium? That turns into prime real estate for Steelers games. A spot behind the 7-Eleven convenience store where Steelers chairman Dan Rooney used to buy coffee and newspapers? Pull in and fire up the grill once you've made sure you are not in a towing zone.

Tailgaters, like a good running back, only need a crack of daylight to turn what looks like nothing into a nice gain. They can also be every bit as meticulous as a coach with their planning and attention to detail.

Experienced tailgaters maximize the space in their vehicle and know how much food and drinks will be needed. They also know exactly when to start shutting down the tailgate so they will be in their seats before opening kickoff. Tailgating seems to bring out the hospitality in people and the added beauty of a tailgate is it can be a few people or swell to a few hundred people.

One tailgate that caught my eye before the Steelers hosted the Broncos less than a week before Christmas in 2015 had just two people but wasn't lacking for anything. It had the requisite grill, one that later would be covered with hamburgers, hot dogs, and chicken wings. And Jason Hupp had also set up a flat-screen TV so he and his family—his wife and daughters were still in their hotel room at the nearby Residence Inn—could watch the early NFL games before heading into Heinz Field.

What drew me to that tailgate more than anything was the sight of Hupp and his young son, Brendan. Each wore a Steelers jersey—No. 43 for dad and No. 7 for son—and they played catch in a lot that had yet to fill with cars.

There is nothing more timeless than a father and son playing catch with a baseball. Right behind that is a father throwing a football to a son who runs fly patterns while imagining he is catching passes inside the packed stadium where he will later cheer his favorite team.

I moved in for a closer look and some questions, ignoring the twinge of guilt I felt for interrupting the game of catch. Jason Hupp, as it turns out, lives in the eastern part of the state and geographically speaking should be an Eagles fan.

But Hupp is a die-hard Steelers fan who brings his family to a game in Pittsburgh every year in what is something of a pilgrimage. He renews his faith in the Steelers and passes that along to his children—even if they are surrounded by Eagles fans in Reading, which is about an hour west of Philadelphia.

"This is more of a home feeling for me culturally," Hupp said of Pittsburgh. "Growing up a Steelers fan I think it's important for my family to experience it."

Steelers fans Jason Hupp, right, and Brendan Hupp at their tailgate prior to the Steelers' final home game in 2015.

The next party I hit could be its own instructional guide on tailgating.

The group has been tailgating in the stadium lot behind the Hyatt Hotel for years and these people don't mess around. I talked to Bob Malnati while he tended to a grill loaded with shrimp and egg rolls, and to borrow one of Steelers coach Mike Tomlin's favorite clichés, this was not his first rodeo.

Bob and his wife, Dow, live in Wexford, a suburb just north of Pittsburgh, and they take charge of the food for the tailgates every year. Bob sets the menu for each game before the season and even posts it online. Breakfast sandwiches, pulled pork, chicken, and Philadelphia cheesesteaks were all main courses during the 2015 season, along with appetizers and a soup du jour.

Bob and Dow, retired teachers who relocated to the Pittsburgh area from upstate New York, charge $10 per person and all they ask is for a head count prior to the game and for any adjustments.

"They have it down to a science," said Jennifer Piper, who lives in upstate New York and has been part of the group for about 10 years. "They bust their butt doing all of this."

Adjustments are necessary because the tailgaters in this group are so friendly that they invariably invite strangers they encounter the night before a game to join them.

They've had visitors from all over the country and the world. During the 2015 season some of the tailgaters met a man from Brazil on Pittsburgh's South Side. He had been in New York with friends who were attending a Giants game and decided he couldn't get that close to Pittsburgh and not go see his beloved Steelers play.

He ended up in Pittsburgh by himself but started talking to some of the tailgaters from this group and joined their party the next day. He is now part of the extended group that stays in touch through social media and it's amazing how easy it is to run into someone from another country at a Steelers game because of the organization's immense popularity.

Such hospitality—Bob and Dow always fly Canadian flags at the tailgate as a sort of Batman signal to Steelers fans north of the border—is only part of the reason why this group of tailgaters does it right. They have fun but don't cross that line where they become obnoxious. They are Steelers fans to the core but don't feel the need to belittle opposing fans.

"You have to respect the other team," Bob said.

Listening to how this group came together is as interesting as hanging out with it before a game. The core members met at the Best Western Hotel in the early 1990s before a game at Three Rivers Stadium. They were all visiting Steelers fans staying at the Best Western and started chatting in the hotel bar.

That encounter morphed into a web of friendships with the Steelers connecting them and not just during the season. They stay in touch throughout the year and even plan a Steelers summer weekend, one in which they get together for a Pirates game.

"We're like a family, and I have Steelers friends for life," said Piper.

No one is more active in the group than Bee Huss.

She is a lifelong Steelers fan despite growing up in northwest Ohio and living in the Toledo area to this day. Bee came of age around the same time the Steelers started winning Super Bowls in the 1970s. She became such a fan that she nervously asked her future husband, Matt, shortly after they met 30 years ago, where his football allegiances lie.

"I've never dated a Cleveland fan and I never would," Bee said. "His exact words were 'I'm a Cincinnati Bengals fan. I [bleeping] hate Cleveland.' I looked at Matt and said, 'I [bleeping] hate Cleveland too.' So we decided to go out. Never in a million years would I have ever thought I would end up marrying a Bengals fan, but we make it work."

All marriages are built on compromise and during the season Bee accompanies Matt to a Bengals game—he is a season ticket holder—and he make a trip to Pittsburgh with her.

He had already fulfilled his commitment by the time the Steelers hosted the Broncos, but Bee's son and grandson were there to take part in her final toast of the season.

Yes, around 90 minutes before kickoff, plastic shot cups are filled and passed around to everyone of age at the tailgate. The concoctions are always friendly—the idea, again, is to have fun and not get someone loaded or sick—and on this day Bee raises her apple pie shot and toasts the people who are friends for life or ones she just made a couple of hours ago.

"We all know how important today is," Bee says, gamely fighting through a cold, which makes it hard to talk. "We've been saying it for the last couple of weeks. Every game is like a playoff game. We're getting relatively healthy and we're doing what we need to do at the right time. I want to be able to hear every one of you from my seat. I want you to come back and be as hoarse as I am right now.

"Enjoy the game, enjoy the atmosphere. Enjoy each other. Have a very safe trip home. It hurts me this is going to be the last home game more than likely but it's been a pleasure spending another season with all of you. Go Steelers and to Bob and Dow for just kicking ass all year."

The toast ends with a collective, "Go Steelers!" and shortly after that Bob and Dow start packing up their vehicle.

I do a second shot with Bee and a few others—hey, it would be rude to turn it down—and am soon on my way. I won't forget this group and I have promised to return the following season.

The two shifts spent with that group—I returned after leaving the first time so I could experience the toast—reinforces to me how ingrained tailgating is in the football culture.

And with good reason.

There are few places where it is easier to check out from the grind of daily life, and tailgates more than anything turn going to a football game into an experience.

Now, I just have to remember to ask Bee what she puts in those purple-colored shots she breaks out every year and calls, "Ravens blood."

Visit a Pittsburgh Institution and Eat a RoethlisBurger

A generation of Steelers fans can talk fondly of walking to Three Rivers Stadium and buying a Peppi's hoagie to take into the game. The iconic sub shop had a near monopoly on fans who didn't tailgate before games, prior to Heinz Field and PNC Park replacing Three Rivers Stadium as the respective homes of the Steelers and Pirates.

The two new stadiums—each tenant started playing in them in 2001—spurred heavy redevelopment on the North Shore, but Peppi's still has four locations in Pittsburgh and it's almost impossible to not run into one of its vendors selling hoagies on the walk to Heinz Field.

Nothing, however, beats visiting the North Shore shop on game days. The line is steady and sometimes out the door but it moves quickly. And Peppi's is one of those places where the food is fresh—they cook everything right in front of you—and everything is good.

Prior to the Steelers' final home game of 2015 a rectangular chalk board outside of Peppi's advertised Lunch Ilkin—a play on the name of Tunch Ilkin, the former Steelers offensive lineman and current color analyst for the team's radio broadcasts.

An Italian hoagie, chips, and a fountain drink for a mere $7.45 is tempting, but there is no way I can walk into Peppi's and order anything but the No. 7, which is also known as the RoethlisBurger.

A couple of bites into my RoethlisBurger, with my arteries cursing me for all they are worth, I realize I didn't need the fresh-cut French fries, as good as they are.

Bee Huss takes front and center near the end of every tailgate she and others faithfully attend before Steelers games at Heinz Field. Huss always provides the toast before people start making their way to the stadium.

Half of the sandwich that is an ode to Ben Roethlisberger will be enough to satisfy both my hunger and curiosity and damn if it isn't as good as the Steelers quarterback.

A mixture of sausage and ground beef make up the foundation of the sandwich and give it a nice little kick. A fried egg and American cheese are also part of it, and mayonnaise, lettuce, and tomatoes can be added as well.

The seeds were planted for the RoethlisBurger shortly after the Steelers selected a sturdy, strong-armed quarterback from Miami (Ohio) with the 11th overall pick in the 2004 NFL draft. The next day one of Jeff Trebac's employees said to him, "RoethlisBurger...hell of a sandwich," and the Peppi's owner started experimenting with different combinations.

He could not have predicted the events that would soon lead to the insatiable demand for the sandwich.

The Steelers' plan to ease Roethlisberger into the NFL changed when an ankle injury suffered by starting quarterback Tommy Maddox in the second game of the season thrust the rookie into action.

Roethlisberger started his first game the following week and won. He won his next start after again leading a fourth-quarter touchdown drive and kept on winning until the end of January.

Roethlisberger became the first NFL quarterback to go 13–0 in the regular season. His emergence turned the sandwich named after him into a Pittsburgh phenomenon. And Root Sports Pittsburgh reporter Dan Potash, after Roethlisberger's second win, told Big Ben about the sandwich and did a story on it.

"By [that] Friday it was in a Florida newspaper," Trebac said. "It exploded."

Indeed, a friend called Trebac after reading about the RoethlisBurger in a Bangkok newspaper, and the alphabet of national TV stations descended on Pittsburgh to chronicle the rise of the quarterback and the sandwich.

A day before the Steelers' game against the New England Patriots on Halloween, Jim Nantz and several CBS TV producers walked into Peppi's. Chris Berman sat down later that season with Roethlisberger at the Steelers' practice facility and each ate a RoethlisBurger. The lunch anchored a five-minute story that ESPN ran on its pre-game shows.

Trebac loved the free advertising but had trouble keeping up with the demand for RoethlisBurgers—and not just when the Steelers were playing at home.

"Every single day it was pandemonium," he said.

It has died down a little, Trebac said, but Roethlisberger and the RoethlisBurger continue to thrive.

"It's not just a novelty," he said. "It's a really, really good sandwich."

Peppi's menu includes other sandwiches named after Steelers players, including the Franco (an Italian sub with extra salami) and the Heath (double steak, onions, peppers, and barbeque sauce).

The special at Peppi's on the day of the Steelers' final home game in 2015 was an ode to Tunch Ilkin. But the big draw at the sub shop is the sandwich named after quarterback Ben Roethlisberger.

Fans who were in the North Shore shop less than three hours before the Steelers and Broncos kicked off probably had two questions about one of the customers: Did Joey Porter order the "Joey Porter Bella"? If so, does the former Steelers outside linebacker and current assistant coach have to pay for the sandwich named after him?

Yes, Porter made a stop at Peppi's before going to work that day at Heinz Field. And try as he might to blend in with the other customers who waited for their orders he simply couldn't. Porter wore dark jeans and a white dress shirt but his barrel chest blew his cover as a former football player. And it's not like Porter blended in when he tormented opposing quarterbacks for the Steelers.

Colorful and occasionally outrageous, Porter became one of the NFL's best pass rushers in the 2000s and one of the faces of the Steelers while playing in Pittsburgh from 1999 to 2006. He was downright quiet, though, as he waited for his sandwich, mindful of the people stealing glimpses of him and politely shaking hands with the customers who wished him and the Steelers luck on their way out of Peppi's.

Porter did order the sandwich named after him—he paid, too, before taking it to go—and it is a mix of grilled steak and portabella mushrooms that is topped with Swiss cheese and spicy horseradish.

Porter was a regular at Peppi's when he played for the Steelers and Trebac knew early on that he approved of the sandwich named after him. After seeing it on the menu for the first time Porter nodded at Trebac as if to say, "Way to go."

Take a Boat Ride to Heinz Field

ailgating can be a production and for those who don't want to deal with the planning, the cooking and the clean-up, here is a suggestion: let someone do it for you.

That is essentially Mark Schiller's pitch with the Ultimate Sailgate Party, a venture he started in 1999 that is much more than just a boat ride to Heinz Field.

The Sailgate ship opens to patrons three hours before kickoff in Pittsburgh's Strip District. A former Steelers player takes part in Sailgate and the first hour is for autographs and photo opportunities as well as eating and drinking.

The meal is catered by Sausalido Restaurant in the Bloomfield section of Pittsburgh and the menu is different for every game. Two hours before kickoff the ship sets sail and there is a one-hour cruise on the rivers that are Pittsburgh's signature.

The ship docks on the Allegheny River, right below Gate A at Heinz Field, and it is a short walk to the stadium. It is open during the game and customers can leave their belongings on the ship. It leaves a half hour after the game is over and stragglers who miss the ship can catch a smaller boat back as it leaves 45 minutes after the end of the game.

The cost is $85 for adults, $65 for seniors and $45 for children under the age of 10. Parking is limited at Sailgate's 23rd Street location but there is a nearby garage that charges a minimal fee relative to parking locations closer to Heinz Field.

The price when factoring in all that comes with Sailgate is more than reasonable, and taking a ride in style to the Steelers game is something worth doing at least once.

"If you don't have a place to tailgate we give you somewhere to hang out," Schiller said. "It's not going to be so crowded you can't move and we try to make it special for you."

The famed Gateway Clipper fleet also provides a nautical option for fans as far as getting to Heinz Field and it leaves from nearby Station Square.

Ships start running three hours before kickoff and depart every 20 to 30 minutes. They also run an hour after the end of games and the cost is $10 round-trip. That does not include parking at Station Square but that expense is generally offset by rates that are less expensive than ones closer to Heinz Field. Also, there are plenty of dining options before and after the game if you take the Gateway Clipper to Heinz Field.

Check out the Scene on the North Shore

A bar scene did not exist on the North Shore when the Steelers played at Three Rivers Stadium. There was the Clark Bar, which occupies the ground floor of a tall brick building topped by the sign with the likeness of the chocolate and peanut butter bar with Pittsburgh roots, and not much else.

Everything changed when Three Rivers closed in 2000. Heinz Field and PNC Park were built and the North Shore was developed. It now

Jerome Bettis's billboard above his restaurant, Grille 36, which is only a couple of blocks from Heinz Field.

offers plenty of bar and restaurant options for fans before and after the game.

No establishment attracts more Steelers fans before a game than Jerome Bettis' Grille 36 Restaurant. Its name and proximity—it is a couple of blocks away from Heinz Field—makes Bettis' a natural spot to which Black and Gold fans gravitate.

I surveyed the scene at Bettis' five-and-a-half hours before the Steelers' game against the Broncos and it was already hopping. Patrons were told that a table in the restaurant came with a 45-minute-to-an-hour wait. The spacious bar was already filled with fans and some were reduced to standing until they could find a seat.

Outside white-hot coals in a grill cooked ribs that had been slathered with barbeque sauce and patrons gathered under a heated tent overlooking the Allegheny River.

Bettis' Grille 36, Tilted Kilt, McFadden's, and Mullen's are among a stretch of bars on the North Shore that swell with Steelers fans long before kickoff and stay packed during and after the game.

There is one caveat when it comes to the eponymous restaurant owned by Bettis: Don't expect to see the Pro Football Hall of Fame running back there before a game.

"I've been there before games and it's a madhouse," Bettis said. "You have a thousand Steelers fans in there and every last one of them wants to see me."

Bettis has always been fan friendly, but he has to draw a line when he is in Pittsburgh if he wants to see more than snippets of the action. "If I'm going to be in town for the game I want to be in the stadium," Bettis said.

Chances are he has the connections to get pretty decent seats.

Take a Picture with "The Chief"

A resplendent life-sized statue of Art Rooney sits on a granite marble bench between Heinz Field and the Allegheny River, not far from where the ships that transport fans to games dock. It is a tranquil site on most days, the Steelers founder immortalized with slicked-back hair and glasses as well as a suit and a signature cigar.

Game days are a different story.

A steady stream of fans pose in front of the statue while pictures are snapped with cameras or cell phones, something that surely would have amused the man affectionately known as "The Chief."

Rooney, who grew up on the North Shore, always prided himself on being a regular person despite his wealth and contributions to Pittsburgh.

The way in which he carried himself still stands out to former Steelers offensive tackle Tunch Ilkin, now the team's color analyst for radio broadcasts, and Ilkin loves telling one story in particular about The Chief.

Ilkin and two other Steelers draft picks were sitting in the lobby of Three Rivers Stadium in the spring of 1982, waiting to talk to Chuck Noll. The three were in Pittsburgh to take physicals and meet with their new head coach when they had a chance encounter with Rooney.

Rooney came bustling through the lobby wearing a cardigan sweater that was missing a button and chewing on one of his stogies. He started straightening up the lobby when he noticed the three players. He gave them a hearty greeting, not dropping even the smallest of hints of his stature, and asked them their names.

Ilkin went first and then one of the other players gave his name and asked Rooney if he was the janitor. Ilkin, who knew that Rooney owned the Steelers, was mortified.

The Chief? Not so much.

"I do a little bit of everything around here," Rooney said with a smile.

Nothing better framed the man than his reaction to a question that might have insulted a lot of team owners.

"You could tell that The Chief was so honored that this young guy thought that he was a regular guy," Ilkin said. "The Chief always used to say, 'Don't be a big shot.' That was kind of his mantra."

That mantra did not stop Arthur J. Rooney from becoming one, although with a common touch that made him a beloved figure in Pittsburgh. Actually, character is more like it since Rooney was one through and through, something that is so eloquently captured in the play *The Chief.*

The play, written by longtime *Pittsburgh Post-Gazette* sports columnist Gene Collier and Rob Zellers, debuted in 2003 and it transcends sports and the Steelers.

It's set in Rooney's office at Three Rivers Stadium and Pittsburgh native Tom Atkins is masterful as The Chief, spinning yarns while waiting to go to a banquet. Woven together through the one-man show, the tales tell not only the story of the Steelers but also the story of Pittsburgh.

The part that will leave Steelers fans with goosebumps comes near the end of the play. As The Chief explains how he missed the greatest play in NFL history, the "Immaculate Reception" is replayed on a screen that has been lowered in the theater and the audience starts cheering.

The second time I saw *The Chief*—and yes, it is worth seeing at least twice—many in the audience were ready for that scene. That is how I

The statue of Steelers
founder Art Rooney
outside of Heinz Field.

HAVE TOWEL, WILL TRAVEL

Terrible Towels travel well and not just within the United States. They have been photographed everywhere from the International Space Station to the top of Mount Kilimanjaro, and taking a picture with the Terrible Towel at a landmark qualifies as a bucket-list item for Steelers fans.

Many have already done it, including Greensburg, Pennsylvania, resident Tim Welty.

Welty, a season-ticket holder for more than 40 years, is among scores of Steelers fans who have a designated traveling Terrible Towel, and he has taken pictures with his towel at the Rock of Gibraltar among other places.

"That towel," he said, "has traveled around the world."

For those who don't travel the world, here is an idea for the Terrible Towel: run a race and wave it as you cross the finish line. The Terrible Towel part is easy. If you need inspiration to actually take part in a race look no further than former Steelers great Alan Faneca.

Faneca has run a marathon, several half marathons, and some trail races since retiring following the 2011 season. Faneca, who played guard for the Steelers from 1998 to 2007, checked in at 315 pounds at his final NFL weigh in and generally played between 315 and 320 pounds. He now weighs around 220 pounds and has become a running enthusiast.

"I've never been this size in my life, at any stage of my life," Faneca said. "I had always said I wanted to lose weight when I was done and it's stuck so far. It's a bad day if I don't get out for a run."

ugly Christmas sweater? Check. Been dying to buy Steelers' Zubaz pants? Check.

I stopped at The Pittsburgh Fan four-and-a-half hours before the Broncos-Steelers game and quickly learned that the aisles of the bustling store are like a sidewalk in New York City: keep moving or risk getting run over.

The store opened at 10:00 AM that day—kickoff wasn't until 4:25 PM—and the shelves behind the register had already been re-stocked by the time I got there around noon. One of the employees had the sole task of folding Terrible Towels, which made sense since 600 to 700 of them are sold before the game.

Surely Myron Cope has to be smiling somewhere when he sees the phenomenon he created with a simple dish towel.

Cope, the legendary Steelers broadcaster and Pittsburgh character, hatched the idea before the Steelers' 1975 playoff game against the visiting Baltimore Colts, albeit somewhat reluctantly. WTAE, the TV station where Cope served as sports director, wanted him to come up with a gimmick to draw more attention to his shows. He went around the Steelers' locker room one day and asked players what they thought of a towel as a prop for fans.

"When he came to me I said, 'Myron, that's a dumb idea, even for you. We don't need our fans waving towels. We need to concentrate on our jobs and not focus on towels being waved,'" former Steelers linebacker Andy Russell said. "I think he just turned around and walked away from me."

Cope apparently got enough support elsewhere for WTAE to go with the Terrible Towel and decades later Russell got an earful about how wrong he had been. Russell, in an interview shown on the Jumbotron at Heinz Field, recounted his initial stance on the Terrible Towel and fans started to boo the former Steelers great.

"No big deal," Russell said with a laugh.

The Terrible Towel has become such a big deal that it is sold in many variations.

Traditional gold towels with black lettering are the most popular ones. But there are also pink towels to promote breast cancer awareness, camouflage towels, and towels for most major holidays, including the Fourth of July.

Proceeds from the sales of Terrible Towels have raised millions of dollars for the Allegheny Valley School in Coraopolis, which serves those with special needs, including Cope's autistic son.

Cope, the longest-tenured broadcaster in Steelers history, passed away in 2008 and hundreds of fans gathered in downtown Pittsburgh soon after his passing to wave Terrible Towels. Cope lives on through the towels that continue to capture the color and energy he supplied to Pittsburgh and the Steelers for so many years.

Opposing players are well aware of what the Terrible Towel means to the Steelers and their fans. Wide receiver T.J. Houshmandzadeh wiped his cleats on a Terrible Towel after scoring a touchdown in the Bengals' 38–31 win at Heinz Field in December of 2005. Three seasons later running back LenDale White jumped up on down on a Terrible Towel with several teammates during the Titans' 31–14 stomping of the Steelers in Nashville.

The Steelers had the last laugh in each case. They knocked the Bengals out of the 2005 playoffs with a win at Cincinnati and watched the top-seeded Titans get upset by the Ravens in the 2008 postseason, paving the way for the Steelers in the AFC. Both seasons they went on to win the Super Bowl.

The most curious case of Terrible Towel dissing came in 2014 when the Steelers visited Jacksonville. The Jaguars' mascot held a Terrible Towel during the game next to a sign that read "Towels Carry Ebola." Jacksonville lost the game and issued an apology for the ill-advised stunt the following day.

POPE YINZER

Dear Father, Art Rooney in Heaven,
Heinz Field be thy name,
Thy kingdom come, and six Super Bowls won,
On Earth, right here in Pittsburgh.
Give us this day, a Primanti sandwich,
And forgive us for our penalties, as we forgive those who try to beat us,
And lead us into the Super Bowl, but deliver us no evil,
For Ben is the kingdom and Troy is the glory, forever and ever. Amen.

Fans who have attended Steelers games at Heinz Field, training camp at St. Vincent College or even rallies in Pittsburgh are no doubt familiar with Don Zadach—or have at least seen him.

That is because Zadach and his wife, Remy, are impossible to miss. Don anointed himself as the "Yinzer Pope" close to 10 years ago, and he wears a homemade mitre with the Steelers logo and drapes himself in black and gold robes and beads as well as Steelers scarves.

Zadach has gained such a measure of fame that he now leads a Steelers prayer at the AE Theater, which is right next to Heinz Field, before every home game. He always delivers the prayer around two hours before kickoff so he and Remy can get to their seats in time for the game.

"I can't go more than a few feet at a time without people stopping me," said Zadach, who lives in Jefferson Township, a South Hills suburb of Pittsburgh.

Not that he ever turns down a photo request, and Zadach takes countless pictures on the day of a game since he and his wife arrive at Heinz Field as tailgaters are setting up in the stadium lots.

The Zadachs visit tailgates in the parking lots outside of Heinz Field and mingle with former Steelers such as Louis Lipps, Barry Foster, and Robin Cole. They also stop at Jerome Bettis' 36 Bar and Grille, McFadden's and

Don Zadach, aka "Pope Yinzer," blessing a fan before a Steelers game.
(Courtesy of Don Zadach)

The Steelers recognized Greene's transcendence in 2014 when they officially retired No. 75 during their November 2 game against the visiting Ravens.

Greene joined Ernie Stautner in receiving the honor and, fittingly, life-sized pictures of the two defensive tackles tower over all else in the FedEx Club on the second level of Heinz Field. Fans who didn't have the opportunity to cheer Greene at halftime of the November 2, 2014, game should pay homage to "Mean Joe" and Stautner and visit this part of the stadium.

"He really was the bedrock, the foundation of our '70s team," Franco Harris said on the night in which the Steelers honored Greene.

Indeed, just as significant as the hiring of head coach Chuck Noll in 1969 was the selection of Greene with the fourth overall pick of the draft that year. The events happened within weeks of one another and started the pivot of a franchise that had just four winning seasons from 1950 to 1968.

Greene possessed great size and his strength remained the stuff of legend long after he had played his last down of football. Just as significant: Greene hated losing and simply would not tolerate it.

The Steelers found that out in the second game of 1969. The Steelers, after winning their opener, trailed the Eagles in Philadelphia and Greene erupted after they failed to convert a fourth down.

He picked up a ball and threw it into the stands, serving notice to his teammates that he would not accept losing.

"He was a great leader," said former Steelers running back Dick Hoak, who played two seasons with Greene and coached on all four Super Bowl–winning teams in the 1970s. "Everybody was afraid of Joe."

Greene's intimidation factor made him the natural leader of the "Steel Curtain," the defensive line that personified the Steelers' domination in the '70s. He formed a tight bond with the other original members of that unit—Ernie "Fats" Holmes, L.C. Greenwood, and Dwight White—and Greene is the only surviving member of that quartet.

That reality—and the death of Noll five months before the jersey retirement ceremony—might have caused Greene to get emotional every bit as much as the sheer magnitude of having his Steelers number officially immortalized.

Greene served a number of other roles in the Steelers organization, from coaching to scouting, and on the night he bid a final farewell to the fans, he was asked how he wanted to be remembered.

"I want them to think that Joe Greene was part of a fantastic football team of the 1970s that probably set the tone and tempo for history for the Pittsburgh Steelers," Greene said. "They helped create what was the most dynamic and fantastic football city and football fans in the world."

Chapter 2

Camping with the Steelers

A Unique Setting and Relationship

WHERE: St. Vincent College in Latrobe, Pennsylvania

WHEN: Late July through at least the middle of August

HOW TO DO IT: Simply block off time on your calendar for training camp. Most of the practices are open and free to the public and parking is free, though it fills up fast.

COST FACTOR: $-$$$$. Steelers fans who live in Western Pennsylvania only need to set aside gas money and cash for food and beverages if they want to make day trips to camp. Out of towners often turn attending training camp into a summer vacation. That can get pricey with lodging, meals, and other entertainment, especially if airfare is involved.

DIFFICULTY FACTOR: This is a definite █. Training camp is as close as fans get to the Steelers and they take advantage of it every summer, showing up in droves and from all over the country. There is a difficulty factor in that big crowds make it harder to do everything from parking close to St. Vincent to getting autographs, but this shouldn't dissuade fans from going. And if you really want to get a sense of the Steelers' national following, walk through the lots one day and count the number of different out-of-state license plates.

· ·

Storm clouds gathered over the Steelers' summer home, confirming an equally ominous weather report, and they forced the grounds crew into action. Tarps were dragged over the fields where the Steelers do their most hitting this side of actual games, and in the rush to beat the rain, Father Benoit Allogia, clad in a black robe, kicked off his sandals and jumped in to help.

Father Paul Taylor watched that scene in 2014, and to him nothing better captures the spirit of cooperation between St. Vincent College and the Steelers. Or the unique relationship between St. Vincent, a small, Benedictine Catholic school nestled in the shadow of the Laurel Highlands, about 30 miles east of Pittsburgh, and the Steelers.

"For Benedictines, our rule says that we are to welcome every guest as Christ himself, so hospitality is paramount," Taylor said, "and in working with the Steelers they have the same value because camp, while it needs to train the players for the season, is also about welcoming fans and giving fans access to an organization."

Indeed, a trip to training camp has to be near the top of a Steelers fan's bucket list because of the access alone. Camp is the best place to get autographs and it is the only time the Steelers open their practices to the public.

Parking and admission are free and there is enough room on the hills overlooking Chuck Noll Field for fans to stake out a good spot to watch practice. The bonus of attending training camp is the unsurpassed setting.

St. Vincent provides panoramic views of the Laurel Valley and surrounding mountains. Just as eye-catching is the sight of Benedictine monks, such as Taylor, watching practice and chatting up players, coaches, and Dan and Art Rooney II.

The uniqueness of Steelers' training camp is such that longtime *Sports Illustrated* NFL writer Peter King once wrote, "On a misty or foggy morning, standing atop the hill at the college, you feel like you're in Scotland. Classic wonderful, slice of Americana. If you can visit one training camp, this is the one to see."

Couldn't agree more. And while you're there, you just might find a few more items to check off your bucket list.

Don't Just Show Up

Camp is all about routine, which is why monotony starts to seep in for the players as the days at St. Vincent turn into weeks. The good part for fans is most of the afternoon practices are open and they run from roughly 3:00 to 5:30 PM, so it's easy to schedule a trip to St. Vincent, which is right off Route 30 in Latrobe.

Fans should prepare for a day at camp and that doesn't just mean showing up with working pens and Sharpies and items to be autographed by the Steelers. Hydrate before arriving at St. Vincent and take water as well as sunscreen with you.

The hotter and more humid the better, as far as Mike Tomlin is concerned, and Mother Nature usually accommodates the Steelers' coach in that department. That makes for a long day for fans, especially younger ones. The best way to maximize the day is to prepare for the worst, from a heat and humidity standpoint, and hope for a cooler summer day. There is a fair amount of walking involved so wear comfortable shoes.

EXTRA POINTS

Jedi Mind Tricks and the Afterlife

Steelers coach Mike Tomlin often wears long-sleeved black shirts during afternoon practices to make a mind-over-matter point to his players in regard to the heat and humidity. Father Paul Taylor wears a black robe with a white collar to practices for a different reason. "I lose a couple of pounds and it's also a good witness," Taylor said. "People see me in long, black robes and the line I use is, 'Do you know why I wear them?' There's one place hotter and I don't want to go there.' So it's an opportunity for evangelization. People think about the afterlife and it's kind of a funny way to do it."

Visit Autograph Alley...If Only to See the Spectacle of It

For anyone who has gone to a Major League Baseball spring training, there are a lot of parallels between it and training camp. The atmosphere is more relaxed—every team is still undefeated—and there is no better opportunity to get close to the players.

That makes autograph alley a must-stop for fans if only to see it.

Autograph alley is a roped-off corridor that runs from St. Vincent's locker room to the football fields. Players pass through the throng of fans on the hillside as they descend the steps that take them to practice.

The Steelers make room at the top of the steps for special-needs children and they make sure rookies know the importance of signing for kids well before the players report to camp. Rookies attend an orientation session at St. Vincent every June and Taylor leads it, showing them around campus and where they can pray or simply find somewhere peaceful to reflect and decompress. Taylor also encourages players to reach out while they are at St. Vincent—and not just during their first season.

"They have an opportunity to sign some autographs and make some fan's day," Taylor said. "There may be a kid struggling with a lot of issues. All of the sudden that kid is a friend to one of the Steelers whom they look up to. That friendship gives that child a reason for hope, a reason to fight, a reason to be happy about something in their

PRANKS ARE PART OF THE FABRIC OF TRAINING CAMP

Kicker Jeff Reed and Steelers head of security Jack Kearney teamed up in 2009 to pull off one of the best pranks in training camp history. The two chartered buses one day near the end of camp and had them parked along a stretch of road that overlooks the football fields. Players couldn't help but see the buses as they made their way to a morning practice. Just as noticeable was their excitement over the anticipation that coach Mike Tomlin would have them stretch and then call it a morning and take the team to the movies. That break never came as Tomlin put the players through a full practice. "It was great," said Doug Whaley, then the Steelers' director of pro personnel. "The players are jumping around having a good warm up, thinking they're going to get out of there and we're all just sitting there laughing." Reed and Kearney had cleared their, ahem, plan with Tomlin and then told everyone else but the players about it. The originality and creativity of the prank left the players laughing about it afterward.

Brett Keisel, meanwhile, made his 12th and final training camp a memorable one for something he pulled off away from the playing fields. Keisel was in a meeting with his fellow defensive linemen when they heard a distinctive roar outside. It came from the Ferrari driven by Lawrence Timmons. And after the linebacker parked it, Keisel decided to take it for a test drive.

"I knew Lawrence was in meetings and maybe his keys were accessible," Keisel said. "He was sitting in a meeting and he heard that car take off because I punched it pretty good. He thought his car had been stolen."

Timmons ran outside where he was informed that Keisel had taken his ride. When Keisel returned, Timmons started giving him the third degree, asking if he had done anything to the car.

"Ship shape," Keisel told Timmons. "I just wanted to see if I wanted to buy one of these."

life, so it's a great opportunity for the players, and the Steelers and the Rooneys look for that opportunity to do that."

Players and coaches sign autographs for fans before practice and after it and most of the established players are good about making time for this. A couple of etiquette suggestions here: if you are an adult, don't push your way in front of a kid if that autograph is for you. Also, don't lose sight of the fact that the players and coaches are there for a job. They can't sign for hours after practice because they have to get treatment, eat dinner, and attend meetings at the end of what is an already long work day.

Watch Practices That Are the Most Spirited of the Year

Simply watching practice is enough for many fans and not just because it is their first glimpse of the Steelers in six months. The pads pop when the players are in full uniform and hitting in some form is a necessity as camp is where whittling a 90-man roster down to 53 and the competition for starting jobs really starts.

The practices are spirited and feature 11-on-11 drills as well as one-on-one competition between different position groups such as receivers vs. defensive backs in passing drills and linebackers vs. running backs in blocking drills.

The best drill at camp is the goal-line competition in which the ball is placed at the 1-yard line and the offense has to score a running touchdown against the defense.

The Steelers do goal-line once or maybe twice during camp and it is never announced beforehand. It could be at the annual Friday practice at Memorial Stadium in nearby Latrobe (more on that night later) or it could be on a Sunday afternoon a week or two into camp with Tomlin wanting to add a charge to practice.

Pittsburgh Steelers coach Bill Cowher, center, shares a laugh with the officials taking part in practice sessions at the team's training camp at St. Vincent College, Friday, August 6, 2004, in Latrobe, Pennsylvania. (AP Photo/Mark Genito)

The goal-line drill is no-holds-barred hitting and tackling and competition at its crackling best, and it turned Isaac Redman into something of a folk hero in 2009. Redman arrived at camp that year as an undrafted free agent out of Bowie State, a Division II school in Maryland.

He distinguished himself as more than just a body at camp by excelling in the two goal-line drills the Steelers held that year, scoring on seven of nine carries.

I'll never forget Redman bulling his way into the end zone repeatedly during his first goal-line drill and then what happened after practice. Reporters flocked to Redman and as he answered questions, Tomlin walked past him on the way to his daily post-practice briefing.

"Sorry to interrupt you, Isaac," the coach said coolly.

Translation: You ain't done squat yet, rookie, so wrap this interview up.

Redman led the Steelers that preseason with 145 rushing yards. After spending a year on the practice squad he played for the Steelers from 2009 to 2013 and rushed for 1,148 yards and five touchdowns during that span.

He scored the decisive touchdown in the final minutes of the Steelers' 13–10 win at Baltimore in 2010, willing his way into the end zone on the nine-yard pass from quarterback Ben Roethlisberger. Without that win, the Steelers wouldn't have gone to the Super Bowl that season, making Redman's rise from obscurity another reason to watch practice.

Nothing stirs the imagination more than seeing a young, unheralded player emerge at camp—and later make a defining play of a season.

Embrace the Legacy of Steelers' Camp at St. Vincent

The Steelers celebrated their 50th anniversary at St. Vincent in 2015 and the history they have there is one aspect that makes training camp so special. The shared experience of living in dorm rooms (with a curfew) and of grinding through padded practices under an unforgiving sun, connects the great teams of the 1970s with the ones that won two Super Bowls and played in another from 2005 to 2010.

Consider that one of former Steelers defensive end Brett Keisel's enduring memories from a career that included two Super Bowl championships involves Joe Greene and training camp.

"I'll never forget being at the same training camp for several years with 'Mean Joe' and he was out there with us every day [as a camp assistant coach]," Keisel said. "That was the coolest thing to me, being able to go out and compete and go to the sidelines and ask him about whatever and him being cool enough to actually try and help you. The greatest ever just watching you trying to carry on the Steel Curtain tradition was a really cool thing. Everyone that got to be around him was better off for it."

Art Rooney II has a Joe Greene training camp story too, but there is a reason why the Steelers president waited for years to actually tell it to "Mean Joe."

It happened when Rooney was young enough to work training camp as a ball boy with Bill Nunn, who later became an actor with a long list of Hollywood credits on his résumé.

"Joe showed up in a beautiful green Lincoln Continental, and somehow Bill got the keys one night and we decided to take it for a ride," Rooney told reporters at the start of 2015 training camp. "We only told Joe that story about 10 years ago. We figured that enough time had passed that we could disclose our little joy ride."

Camp has produced countless stories such as that one over five decades. It also gave birth to the legend of Greene.

In 1969, Greene arrived to training camp a day after it started because of a contract dispute. The Steelers had selected Greene with the fourth overall pick and that alone would have made the defensive tackle a target at camp. When he showed up late it really rankled some of the veteran players, especially center Ray Mansfield.

First-year coach Chuck Noll did not ease Greene into camp, quickly tabbing him for the famed Oklahoma drill. The Oklahoma drill pits an offensive lineman and a running back against a defensive player, who has to beat a block and get the back on the ground. Mansfield, who would play 11 seasons for the Steelers and start on their first two Super Bowl teams, made sure he got the first crack at Greene.

EXTRA POINTS

Gone But Not Forgotten

Brother Patrick Lacey, a fixture at training camps for five decades, didn't just serve as a key groundskeeper after the Steelers made St. Vincent College their permanent summer home. Brother Pat did a little bit of everything at St. Vincent, serving as the campus fire chief as well as its bowling coach among other things. Brother Pat was a member of a handful of firefighting associations locally and throughout the state. He also coached bowling from 1970 to 1981 and led St. Vincent to an NAIA national championship in 1978. Lacey became close with the Rooneys and the Steelers wrote an obituary for the team website after Brother Pat passed away in 2010 at the age of 79. "Such a good man, such a prayerful guy," Father Paul Taylor said. "He loved mowing that lawn and he was a plumber so if something went wrong in the dorm he had to be there."

The Steelers moved all over the place for camp before settling at St. Vincent for good in 1966.

They spent summers in Rhode Island and at West Liberty College in West Virginia, where water buffaloes were sometimes needed to keep the fields from overcooking in the heat. The Steelers also trained closer to home at Slippery Rock University and Carnegie Mellon University, and, as Art Rooney Jr. put it, "We moved around like a bunch of gypsies."

That changed due to the friendship between Art Rooney and Art Rooney Jr. and Oland "Dodo" Canterna.

Canterna played basketball and baseball at Pitt and excelled at both. The Freeport, Pennsylvania, native scored 857 points in a career that spanned from 1944 to '49 and he left Pitt as its all-time leading scorer. Canterna also distinguished himself in baseball and played three seasons in the Boston Braves' organization before accepting two head-coaching positions at St. Vincent in 1954.

Art Rooney regularly attended Pitt sporting events and he gave players tickets to Steelers games at Forbes Field. He got to know Canterna through this and the two became friends.

Canterna got to know Art Rooney Jr. when the latter attended St. Vincent and played football there. His relationship with the Rooneys made Canterna the perfect point man when the Steelers wanted to establish a permanent training camp away from Pittsburgh but also close to home.

The Steelers had practiced periodically at St. Vincent College when they moved around and liked its proximity to Pittsburgh. Canterna was all for the Steelers making St. Vincent their summer home, but the school's president, Rev. Maynard Brennan, knew nothing about football.

Canterna and St. Vincent chemistry professor Bill Dzombak, a big Steelers fan, sold the idea to Brennan, who had to be naturally skeptical about turning the small, bucolic campus over to an NFL team for most of July and August.

"He said, 'We'll see what happens. If it goes right, fine,'" Canterna said.

The Steelers also had to adopt a wait-and-see approach to St. Vincent. The school had discontinued football after the 1962 season and its fields had fallen into disrepair—at least by the standards for NFL teams.

"They were okay for intramurals," Art Rooney Jr. recalled.

Rocks littered the fields and removing them proved to be one of the biggest tasks facing the Steelers and St. Vincent. Whipping the fields into shape fell in large part on Steelers equipment manager Jack Hart.

He worked with St. Vincent on that basic requirement and sometimes took boys to the campus so they could pick up rocks and pull weeds. But the Steelers did more than just pay some pocket money to teenagers to get the fields ready for training camp.

They eventually dug up the fields and planted new soil. Brother Pat Lacey took ownership of the fields and his caretaking helped make him a training-camp fixture.

"Every night he watered the field," Canterna said, "and the grass started coming up real nice."

The Steelers, meanwhile, proved to be a big hit at St. Vincent. Canterna said it was common for them to draw 10,000 people for scrimmages and the symbiotic relationship that the Steelers and St. Vincent enjoy today has its roots in the early cooperation between the two sides.

"They made a lot of friends and we made a lot of friends," Canterna said in late January of 2016. "I enjoyed every minute of it."

The players do not enjoy every minute of training camp. That is why former Steelers running back Jerome Bettis chose his words carefully when I asked him about St. Vincent.

"It was nice...for training camp," Bettis said. "That's the one part we hated the most was going to training camp. Having to be up there for a couple of weeks, it was never fun. We made fun out of it but it was never really fun."

Bettis rarely if ever pondered the uniqueness of St. Vincent when he played for the Steelers or marveled at the spectacular views its campus offers because camp is nothing if not a grind. The players return to their college roots when they check into camp and promptly move into a dorm room where they will live for anywhere from close to three weeks to a month.

They are bound to that room at a designated time every night by curfew. The days, meanwhile, are regimented and start to bleed into one another because the routine is largely the same. The shared experience of camp is essential to team building, even if it lacks basic comforts—perhaps because it lacks basic comforts.

"Getting away is good, I think," said former Steelers guard Alan Faneca, who spent 10 training camps at St. Vincent. "I equate it to people and tell them 'Think of spending four weeks every year in some dorm room, away from everything that you have, the whole family, your possessions, your favorite chair in the living room, everything, and that adds up.' I played 13 years so I spent a little over a year in training camp. It's kind of crazy once you say it like that."

Almost as crazy is that this current group of Steelers players has it considerably easier at camp than their predecessors. Two-a-day

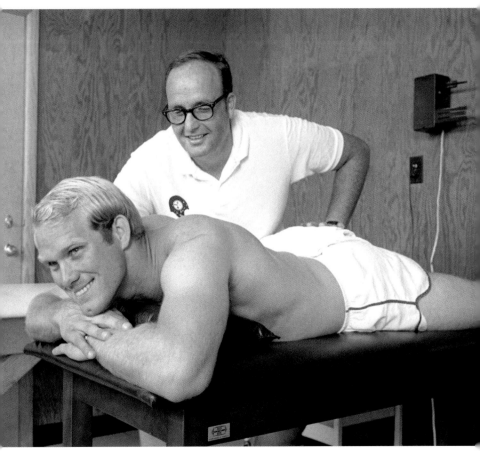

Terry Bradshaw, the No. 1 overall pick of the 1970 NFL Draft, gets treatment from Steelers trainer Ralph Berlin at rookie camp in 1970 at St. Vincent's College in Latrobe, Pennsylvania. (AP Photo/Harry Cabluck)

practices, once a staple of camp, are a thing of the past because of the collective bargaining agreement.

The current players have it better in other ways, too.

The dorm rooms are air-conditioned, a luxury that players didn't have for the first three decades at St. Vincent, and there is more room for the Steelers as a whole because of the growth of the campus.

Jason Gildon, the Steelers' all-time sacks leader, joined the team in 1994 as a third-round draft pick from Oklahoma State. He said the dorms did not have air conditioning until his third season. Gildon also recalled the offenses and defenses meeting in one big room separated only by a partition.

"It's come a long way from when I was there," said Gildon, who played 10 seasons for the Steelers. "Going back and seeing how much it's grown and how much it's expanded, it's amazing."

Yet the tableau remains largely the same, which is part of St. Vincent's allure, especially for the fans.

They return every year knowing where to park, knowing the best places to stake out spots for autographs and to watch practice.

Father Paul Taylor said one of his favorite parts of training camp is watching fans interact with the coaches and players. St. Vincent's chief liaison to the Steelers gets to know his share of fans too. They come from all over the United States and from out of the country as well. Camp is filled with locals too and Taylor always knows where to find a couple from nearby Greensburg. The husband and wife watch practice every day from under the same maple tree that overlooks the football fields.

"I get the best scouting report from them," Taylor said. "They're here every day and I'm sure they're not alone."

All signs indicate that fans will be attending training camp at St. Vincent for years to come. The 50th anniversary celebration in 2015

The 9/11 monument to heroism and patriotism is less than an hour from Latrobe and the drive east on Route 30 is a scenic one that winds through quaint hamlets like Ligonier and Jennerstown.

The memorial gives folks to a chance to pay their respects to the 33 passengers and seven crew members who took down a hijacked flight in an obscure field. Terrorists intended to fly to Washington D.C. but they were overwhelmed by passengers and crew who made the ultimate sacrifice for their country and took down the plane.

"It really makes a deep impact on visitors," said MaryJane Hartman, chief of interpretation and visitors services at the Flight 93 National Memorial. "That memory is so imprinted in their mind that they relive that day. We get every emotion."

Admission to the memorial is free and during camp it opens at 9:00 AM and doesn't close until 7:00 PM. Donations are accepted and visitors often leave tributes to the fallen heroes.

A new visiting center opened in September of 2015 and visitors can walk along the path of the plane before it crashed and learn about the people on the doomed flight.

Their stories are on display, and most poignant are three final phone calls made to loved ones when they knew the plane was getting taken down. Those recordings are available at the memorial, making more breathtakingly real the surreal events of September 11, 2001.

Hartman said the Flight 93 memorial drew 300,000 visitors annually even before the addition of the visitors' center. The site, she said, gets a significant amount of traffic during Steelers' training camp.

Make time for this visit if you are coming from out of the area for training camp and appreciate the sacrifices so many have made for this country.

That includes Steelers and two stand out in particular.

Rocky Bleier, who was drafted by the Army after playing his rookie season with the Steelers in 1968, sustained serious injuries to each of his legs while fighting in the Vietnam War. He lost part of his right foot and doctors told Bleier he would never play football again.

Bleier, who was awarded a Bronze Star and Purple Heart for bravery, fought his way back and by 1974 he had established himself as a starter with Franco Harris in the Steelers' backfield. He proved to be an excellent complement to Harris and won four Super Bowls with the Steelers. His story inspired Bleier to write a book, and *Fighting Back: The Rocky Bleier Story* was turned into a TV movie, a lot of which was shot at St. Vincent College.

Steelers offensive tackle Alejandro Villanueva has authored a tale almost as unlikely as Bleier's. Villanueva played a handful of different positions at Army, including wide receiver. He served three tours in Afghanistan after graduating from West Point and becoming an Army Ranger and received a Bronze Medal for Valor and other commendations for his service.

Villanueva went to training camp with the Eagles in 2013 as a defensive end but didn't stick. The Steelers signed Villanueva to their practice squad after the Eagles waived him, and converted the 6'9", 320-pounder to offensive tackle.

He made the 53-man roster in 2015 and protected quarterback Ben Roethlisberger's blind side after starting left tackle Kelvin Beachum went down with a knee injury.

Villanueva, who is in the Army Reserves, fittingly emerged as one of the unsung heroes on a team that won its first playoff game since the 2010 season and almost advanced to the AFC Championship Game.

Chapter 3

Going Deep on the Steelers' Bucket List

Attend Steelers Fantasy Camp and This Isn't Just For the Men

WHERE: Pittsburgh and Latrobe

WHEN: Men's fantasy camp is held every year in early June; women's camp is held during training camp in late July.

HOW TO DO IT: Keep an eye on the Steelers' team website (www.steelers.com). The schedule and events section of the site keeps fans informed about what is coming up on the calendar. Register as early as possible for events such as these as they generally sell out. Information is also available by calling (412) 697-7713.

COST FACTOR: $$$–$$$$. The Steelers' fantasy experiences are reasonably priced but most out of towners have the added expense of airfare.

DIFFICULTY FACTOR: ▮ If you have the money and register early there will be a spot for you.

BUCKET RANK: 🪣🪣🪣🪣🪣

. . . .

Attending a game at Heinz Field and seeing the team up close at training camp is a good start for Steelers fans, especially with all that comes with each experience. But there is still a ton to do and we stay mostly in the Pittsburgh area in this chapter for bucket-list items with a couple of notable exceptions.

Steelers' fantasy camp for men, what might qualify as cruel and unusual punishment for a Ravens fan, is held annually the weekend after Memorial Day when St. Vincent College is starting to get its campus ready for training camp.

Fantasy camp participants arrive in Pittsburgh—most fly into the area—on a Friday and are given a tour of Heinz Field. From there they head to St. Vincent, where they experience training camp, albeit on a different scale than the regular players.

The first night they attend a reception that features alumni players and a Hall of Fame induction ceremony.

Yes, those attending their fifth consecutive camp are enshrined in the Steelers' men's fantasy camp Hall of Fame. Those attending their 10th camp overall receive prizes and tickets as well as a pair of pre-game sideline passes to a mutually agreed upon game.

The real action starts Saturday and it isn't just a bunch of twenty-somethings running around, trying to emulate a favorite Steelers player or relive their glory days.

"We've got guys in their early seventies that come up here," Steelers marketing manager of events John Simpson said.

All participants are put through a morning and afternoon practice on Saturday and there are six different stations, three for offense and three for defense.

Bridging the practices are lunch and a Q&A session with a Steelers coach. That night a banquet is held in the dining hall that includes a prime-rib dinner and guest speaker. In 2015, newly minted Pro Football Hall of Famer Jerome Bettis was the featured speaker at camp.

A skills competition is held on Sunday in lieu of a flag-football game and there are different age groups to level the playing field since the minimum age to participate is only 23. Camp closes with lunch and a ceremony in which participants receive a Steelers jersey—black and white are given in alternate years—and a gift bag.

Fantasy camp is often the start of friendships between men who would have never met if not for their love of the Steelers.

"There's guys from Vancouver, British Columbia, that are now buddies with guys from Louisiana and they met at Steelers camp," Simpson said. "They all have their stories and Steelers rooms. It's a lot of work but it's a blast to put on with the guys."

It's a blast too for Steelers fans like Skip Brown.

Brown is in the fantasy camp Hall of Fame, and he has attended nine of them since his first one in 2004.

"It's a Steelers fan's dream come true," said Brown, who is in his upper fifties and lives in the Pittsburgh suburb of Whitehall. "You get to interact with present and past Steelers and it really makes you appreciate the game and what these guys go through."

Brown may be more equipped to handle the physical rigors of fantasy camp than most because of his background as an athlete. The 6'10", 300-pounder—yes, you read that right—played college basketball at Davidson, the school Steph Curry put on the map.

His time in North Carolina never dulled Brown's love for the Steelers and his family has had season tickets for more than 50 years. Brown's father owned a grocery store in Castle Shannon and former Steelers cornerback and Pro Football Hall of Famer Jack Butler shopped there frequently and became a good friend of the family.

Brown later befriended former Steelers defensive end Dwight White through his line of work in computer software. Both were frequently on the same flights to and from Pittsburgh and found themselves seated next to one another in the exit row because of the extra leg room.

Brown has gotten to know more former Steelers players through fantasy camp. He has also made friends with Steelers fans he never would have met if not for fantasy camp.

"What's really neat is I meet people from far away," Brown said. "There's people that come from Mexico and they come from just about every state in the union."

. . . .

Something For the Ladies Too

The Steelers are well aware that male fans aren't the only ones who will pay to experience Black and Gold football beyond going to the games or watching them on TV.

The Steelers host three events annually that cater to their female fans. All of them, Simpson said, sell out and offer an inside glimpse at the organization.

Every training camp the Steelers host a day for women that includes instruction from alumni, meals, sideline passes to an afternoon practice and an autograph session with select current players. The one-day camp is often wrapped into an extended visit to Steelers training camp, and Simpson said it typically draws women from between 20 to 25 different states.

Also popular is ladies' night at Heinz Field, which includes drills run by alumni—the women can participate in as much of that aspect of the night as they want—and a prime-rib dinner in one of the Heinz Field club lounges. Two current players attend the event and talk about what a typical day is like for them during the season.

The third event for females only is called Women's 202 and it provides the best behind-the-curtain look at the Steelers. It is staged during the season at the UPMC Rooney Complex, where the Steelers practice, and an assistant coach talks Xs and Os with the ladies to give them a better understanding of the game.

Three current players put them through drills at the indoor practice facility and sign autographs. The night also includes a tour of the Steelers' locker room and photo opportunities with the six Super Bowl trophies on the second floor of the facility.

THESE STEELERS CAN HOOP

Brett Keisel and Charlie Batch suited up for more than a decade for the Steelers and each also played his share of hoops on the Steelers' basketball team. I asked each for his starting five among those he played with over the years. I did not give Keisel the option of picking five other than himself since everyone who has seen him play basketball knows how good he is.

Team Batch:

Brett Keisel

Ben Roethlisberger

Antwaan Randle-El

Deshea Townsend

Santonio Holmes

Team Keisel:

Roethlisberger

Randle-El

Ike Taylor

Max Starks

Hoop It Up Against the Steelers Footballers— or At Least Watch

WHERE: Select Steelers players travel the tri-state area of Pittsburgh, playing against different teams in fundraisers.

WHEN: The Steelers' basketball team plays in the spring when the players are back in Pittsburgh lifting and working out and later taking part in off-season practices.

HOW TO DO IT: Call (412) 697-7713 to get information on scheduling a game against the Steelers. They generally play against faculty from a high school or police and fire departments so don't put a team together thinking the Steelers are going to come play against you unless you have access to a gym.

COST FACTOR: $$–$$$. Tickets to watch the game are inexpensive but it will cost some money to play against the Steelers. Both sides, however, make out on the game as each raises money for their respective charities.

DIFFICULTY FACTOR: ▮ The Steelers play a limited number of games within a limited time period.

BUCKET RANK:

Those looking to test themselves athletically against Steelers players can do so every spring. The Steelers field a touring basketball team that gives fans a chance to see them up close albeit in a different sporting venue.

Sometimes those fans get too much of a good look at the Steelers as an overeager hoopster found out one year against former Steelers defensive end Brett Keisel.

Keisel is 6'5" and can shoot the rock as well as handle it. He earned *Parade* and McDonald's honors as player of the year in Wyoming as a high school senior and could have played Division I college basketball had he pursued that sport instead of football.

The Steelers games come with the basic understanding that it is fine to compete while keeping in mind that no NBA scouts are in the stands.

Keisel found himself matched up against a player one game who did not grasp this or simply wanted to show up a Steelers player on the hardwood.

"[Keisel] kept saying, 'Calm down,'" former Steelers quarterback Charlie Batch recalled with a laugh. "He wouldn't calm down and Brett said, 'You know what? Screw this.' He ended up driving the lane and dunking on him and said, 'You want to keep playing? I got you.' The rim was shaking and everyone was like, 'Holy crap!'"

Keisel's take on this?

"There were a couple of occasions like that where you'd play against some people and they wanted to show us up," Keisel said. "Sometimes as a competitor your juices start flowing too and of course you're not going to back down."

Keisel once had to remind himself to dial it down after dunking on a girl when the Steelers played a team of faculty members.

"After I did it I took myself out of the game and was like, 'What am I doing? I'm taking this way too serious,'" he said. "Sometimes you just get competitive."

Situations like that, however, are the exception and not the rule.

The Steelers play to the crowd, whether it is someone like James Harrison launching half-court shots or players pulling kids out of the stands to shoot free throws for them.

The games, Batch said, are always a good time for fans, who get to see Steelers players in a generally relaxed and fun atmosphere.

"Here you are in the gymnasium and you're 10 feet away from [Steelers players] and you're able to take pictures with guys at halftime," Batch said. "Guys love that and when you see the reaction of some of these kids, that's what it's about."

Batch's knees don't allow him to play more than short stretches when he suits up for the Steelers' hoops squad. But Batch, a deadeye shooter, proudly claims to have set an unofficial team record when the Steelers played a game at Valley High School in New Kensington, which is just outside of Pittsburgh.

"I made 22 threes and Ben Roethlisberger witnessed that," Batch said, adding that the Steelers scored 150 points in four eight-minute quarters. "That was a good day for me."

MIKE TOMLIN PULLED THE ULTIMATE TRUMP CARD TO QUELL CONTROVERSY

The Lombardi trophies that line the front of the Steelers' library symbolize what coach Mike Tomlin means when he says, "The standard is the standard." When I think of the Lombardi Trophies I am reminded of how Tomlin headed off a potential problem in his second season.

Starting running back Willie Parker, in the midst of a frustrating season, griped after practice late in the season that the Steelers had gotten away from their identity and needed to re-examine their approach to the ground game.

Offensive coordinator Bruce Arians, who never had much use for a traditional fullback, was scheduled to address reporters the following day. Tomlin instead met with reporters in the Steelers' media room, which is right around the corner from the library, and absolutely squashed the potential controversy.

"Every morning I come to work I walk past five Lombardi Trophies, not five rushing titles," Tomlin said. "The issue for us has been, is and hopefully will continue to be, winning. That's my interpretation of Steelers football."

The Steelers added a sixth Lombardi a couple of months later and not because of the message Tomlin sent. His unequivocal response to Parker's critique did reinforce that the head coach, only 36 years old at the time, was clearly in control of a veteran team.

Pittsburgh Steelers head coach Mike Tomlin celebrates after his team's 27-23 win over the Arizona Cardinals in Super Bowl XLIII, Sunday, February 1, 2009, in Tampa, Florida.

(AP Photo/David J. Phillip)

Check Out the Steelers' Practice Facility and "Unite" With the Team

WHERE: Pittsburgh, Pennsylvania

WHEN: Any time, though the facility is not open to the public.

HOW TO DO IT: Go to Pittsburgh's South Side and the facility is just off South Water Street.

COST FACTOR: This one is free.

DIFFICULTY FACTOR: ◖ It is easy to get close to the facility for fans who just want a peek at where the Steelers spend the most time as far as their homes. Getting in is another question as tours are limited.

BUCKET RANK: 🗑🗑🗑🗑

The Steelers' practice facility runs along the Monongahela River, not far from the Hot Metal Bridge, and fans seeking autographs or trying to catch a glimpse of practice have a limited opportunity to do both.

I don't recommend staking out the street leading into the facility as players aren't going to stop their car and sign autographs. Practices, meanwhile, are closed to the public and the fence framing the practice fields and accompanying tarp don't allow for sight lines. If you are content to listening to practice, have at it—and with Steelers fans you never know.

The biggest draw of the facility that the Steelers share with the Pitt Panthers is the library on the second floor. Six gleaming Lombardi Trophies stand behind a large glass window and coaches pass them on the way to their offices. They are a powerful sight and definitely worth seeing.

Those who don't have the connections to get a tour of the facility have the opportunity to do so through Steelers Nation Unite.

The organization started the initiative in October, 2015, and it uses technology to connect fans from all over the world with the Steelers and each other. Membership is free and is consummated in mere minutes after going to www.steelersnationunite.com. Steelers fans would be crazy not to take advantage of it.

Steelers Nation Unite does a little bit of everything to bring fans closer to the team. It regularly stages conference calls with Steelers players, past and present, as well as others in the organization. Ben Roethlisberger, Antonio Brown, Jerome Bettis, John Stallworth, and Lynn Swann were among those who took part in the weekly calls during the 2015 season.

"We try to give that insider access," said Michael "Ponch" Hustava, Steelers Nation Unite marketing coordinator. "The biggest thing is to try to keep it fresh."

Steelers Nation Unite does that for home games—and away from Heinz Field.

Members attending games simply have to RSVP by sending a text alert to Steelers Nation Unite. That qualifies them for prizes that include pregame field passes and participation in the Terrible Towel twirl as well post-game field passes and photo opportunities.

During the Steelers' 45–10 win over the Indianapolis Colts on December 6, 2015, two members of Steelers Nation Unite were presented with an upcoming trip to Cleveland that included tickets and transportation in a limousine. When the Steelers held their annual reunion weekend three weeks earlier against the Browns, Casey Hampton, Brett Keisel, and James Farrior were among those who surprised Steelers Nation Unite members in their seats with signed jerseys from Super Bowl XL.

Steelers Nation Unite is also active on the road.

It seeks out Steelers fans for road games and delivers Terrible Towels among other things to tailgates. It also gathers fans the night before games at Steelers bars, something it did in San Diego and Seattle.

The San Diego gathering attracted around 400 fans as well as special guest and Pro Football Hall of Famer Dermontti Dawson, who lives in that area. The Seattle party also packed the place and fans went nuts when Steelers Nation Unite snuck Keisel into the bar through a back door.

NO FOOLING CHUCK NOLL

Frenchy Fuqua joined the Steelers in 1970 via a trade with the New York Giants, and he learned early that it was tough to pull one over on coach Chuck Noll. The night before a home game the Steelers were lodging at the Roosevelt Hotel in Pittsburgh and Fuqua decided to have his fiancé stay in his room past the 10:00 PM curfew.

He told her to hide in the shower when Noll knocked on his door with a request to use Fuqua's stereo. Fuqua nervously obliged and Noll listened to one song before heading for the door. Just as Fuqua was about to exhale, Noll walked into the bathroom and pulled back the shower curtain. "Madam," he said, "you have to leave. This man has to work tomorrow." Noll didn't follow through on fining Fuqua, as he said he would do, but the second-year coach made his point. "I never attempted that again," Fuqua said with a laugh.

Steelers Nation Unite is still evolving—and will continue to adapt to emerging technology—but it is already such a success that it has members from more than 110 countries, Hustava said.

This is an easy one to check off on a Black and Gold bucket list and the mere minutes it takes to become a member is well worth it for Steelers fans of all stripes.

. . . .

Take a Picture With Franco Harris' "Immaculate Reception" Statue

WHERE: Pittsburgh International Airport in Moon Township

WHEN: Anytime

HOW TO DO IT: Make a quick stop and take a picture

COST FACTOR: This one is free

DIFFICULTY FACTOR: 🗑 There really is none unless you are rushing to catch a flight.

BUCKET RANK: 🗑🗑🗑🗑🗑

. . . .

Two life-sized statues stand sentry at the airside elevators inside of Pittsburgh International Airport, and scores of passengers stop to shoot pictures or at least take an extended look at them on a daily basis.

it eventually and all I'd wind up with is different colored sand in the shoe."

Fuqua played in an era where Astroturf was prevalent—and the equivalent of playing on green concrete. But his feet hurt him today, above all else, because of the platform shoes.

"My feet are terrible," Fuqua said. "I go every six weeks to the foot doctor. I don't know how women walk with high heels."

That observation is followed by a gregarious laugh and that laugh is usually just around the corner when Fuqua is telling stories about the "Immaculate Reception," how he made peace with some of the Oakland Raiders players in that game, including Tatum, and the time coach Chuck Noll caught him with his fiancé in a hotel room after curfew.

But Fuqua can also tackle more serious issues such as managing concussions, how that has evolved and how dangerous the game has become even with league initiatives to make it safer.

"The NFL has a long way to go and the reason it has a long way to go is you are re-teaching the whole philosophy of the game," Fuqua said. "Hell, everyone from the '60s through the '80s, they were taught that you use your head as a weapon. You've seen the cartoons when a guy gets hit with a hammer and stars pop up in his head? I have seen the stars and went back in and played."

The sobering reality, Fuqua said, is that serious injuries—and health issues later in life—are inevitable with players only getting bigger and faster.

"I could not have played in the NFL over the last 20 years," said Fuqua, who rushed for 3,031 yards and 21 touchdowns in 100 career NFL regular-season games. "The guys are humongous. We had some tough S.O.B.s but these guys today are like animals and they work out 365 days a year. I am frightened for the NFL player today."

More—much more—on concussions later.

Visit "Franco's Italian Army" Headquarters For a Good Meal and Some History

WHERE: Vento's Pizza in the East Liberty section of Pittsburgh

WHEN: Vento's has regular hours though it is closed on Sunday

HOW TO DO IT: Just show up at a reasonable hour Monday through Saturday

COST FACTOR: $-$$. Get a pizza but also try the sandwich named after Franco Harris. There is no shame at all in walking out of Vento's with leftovers.

DIFFICULTY FACTOR: ▊ There is none.

BUCKET RANK: 🗑️🗑️🗑️🗑️🗑️

Vento's Pizza, situated in a shopping center anchored by a Home Depot, can seem unremarkable to motorists passing by on busy North Highland Avenue. A closer look, however, reveals it to be a must-stop for Steelers fans.

The first clue that the place is an absolute treasure is the window with the sign that touts Vento's as "Home of Franco's Italian Army." Step inside and step back into time.

The restaurant only accepts cash and a sign on the soda fountain advises patience since everything is made to order. It is the kind of place where you can't go wrong ordering anything, and the steaming Sicilian pies feature a thick crust that melts in your mouth. The wait for the pizzas is as worthwhile as the pies themselves since Vento's could also qualify as a Steelers museum.

The restaurant walls are covered with photographs and memorabilia that document that Steelers' history, from a 1933 picture of the first team (then called the Pittsburgh Pirates) to one of founder Art Rooney posing with four Lombardi Trophies.

Framed *Sports Illustrated* covers highlight two of the most celebrated grabs in Super Bowl history. There is the one of Lynn Swann near the end of the ridiculous catch against the Dallas Cowboys, the one in which he tipped the ball to himself several times as he was falling down before making a catch in Super Bowl X. To the right of that indelible Super Bowl highlight is the shot of John Stallworth making the iconic over-the-shoulder grab that allowed the Steelers to overcome the Los Angeles Rams and win their fourth Super Bowl.

The pictures stir all kinds of memories, and the past really comes to life when the patriarch of Vento's ambles into the restaurant he has owned since 1951. Al Vento meets every Saturday with a group that includes brothers John, a World War II veteran who fought in the Pacific theater, and Andy. And on a crisp November day in 2015, Vento, who was 89 years old at the time, talked about one of his most cherished creations: Franco's Italian Army.

Vento and the late Tony Stagno founded the most famous of fan clubs that sprouted when the Steelers started winning big. "The Army," as Vento still calls it, is as much a part of 1970s lore as the Terrible Towel.

What eventually became the most famous standing army in Western Pennsylvania since George Washington's troops fought there started when Vento and Stagno asked Steelers guard Sam Davis, a frequent customer at Vento's, about doing something to celebrate Harris' Italian heritage.

Harris loved the idea of an Italian army when they pitched it to him, and to say Vento and Stagno ran with it is an understatement. They had a friend in the Army Reserves get them helmets and The Italian Army went so far as to ride tanks onto the field at Three Rivers Stadium before one game against the hated Raiders. They even dropped leaflets announcing their arrival. They had made an arrangement with the Steelers about the tanks but could not convince the weather to also cooperate and strong winds caused the leaflets to miss their drop.

Al Vento, left, and Tony Stagno, right, initiate Frank Sinatra into Franco's Italian Army in a picture that hangs in Vento's Pizza in Pittsburgh.

"They blew everywhere but onto the field," Vento recalled with a chuckle. "It was a fun era and I don't think it will ever be duplicated."

Indeed, imagine a fan club driving *anything* onto an NFL field these days with the state of security. Or sneaking bags of wine into the game.

The Italian Army did both, cutting out the inside of loaves of bread from Stagno's bakery and tucking Riunite bottles into the hollowed parts. They only had to get past one security guard in those days and a chaplain distracted the guard while the Army carried the bags of supplies to their seats on the 30-yard line. There they ate hoagies, waved Italian flags and toasted the Steelers as well as Myron Cope in the broadcast booth.

Cope, as colorful a character as Pittsburgh has ever produced, had embraced the Army from its inception, and the legendary broadcaster played a key role in its most famous moment.

Cope was dining in a Palm Springs restaurant known for feeding the stars in 1972 as the Steelers were practicing in Southern California in advance of their regular-season finale at San Diego.

Cope saw Frank Sinatra and had a waiter deliver a note on a napkin asking the legendary singer to join the army. As Cope later told Ed Bouchette of the *Pittsburgh Post-Gazette*, he played up Harris' Italian heritage and even said he was from Hoboken, New Jersey—Sinatra had been born there—when in fact Harris was from southern New Jersey.

Cope's machinations worked. He convinced Sinatra to attend Steelers practice the following day and phoned Vento and Stagno with orders to fly to California at once.

Jim Boston, the Steelers' traveling secretary, had naturally been skeptical of Cope's claim that Sinatra would show at practice and teased Cope about it the next day. "Out of the blue," Vento recalled,

"Frankie taps [Boston] on the shoulder and says, 'When I make an appointment I keep it.'"

Adding to the surreal scene was Chuck Noll, the stern coach who hated distractions, ordering Harris to take a break from practice so he could attend Sinatra's induction into the army.

"We made him a colonel," Vento said with a laugh.

As Vento talked a picture of him and Stagno with Sinatra hung not more than a goal-line plunge behind him, adding visual proof to a story that sounds too good to be true.

Those were different times in a different era and Vento savored every one of them. The army commissioned a division of Steelers fans from Butler, which is north of Pittsburgh, and it even marched in the stadium when the Steelers played at Cleveland.

"A couple of times they wanted to fight us," Vento said of the Browns fans, "but we took care of ourselves. We didn't walk away feeling bad, I'll tell you that."

Vento keeps in touch with Harris and his wife, Dana, and he still has Steelers season tickets though he usually only attends the first two home games of the year while the weather is still warm.

Franco's Italian Army has long disbanded but Vento and his restaurant keep it alive. Vento's is worth visiting for the food and atmosphere alone. An added bonus is listening to Al Vento spin tales from a bygone era.

"The '70s and '80s were the greatest fan clubs and fun we ever had and the teams were good," he said. "All good things have to come to an end."

Sailing the High Seas with the Steelers

WHERE: Steelers cruises leave from Florida.

WHEN: This is a relatively new event and it was held in late February in 2016.

HOW TO DO IT: Go to www.legendsofpittsburghcruise.com for information, including dates and how to register.

COST FACTOR: $$$-$$$$ The base cost is well under $1,000 but add-ons can be purchased and airfare is not included.

DIFFICULTY FACTOR: ▌ If you are willing to pay there is probably going to be a spot for you since cruise ships aren't getting any smaller. Like with the fantasy camps, though, keep an eye on registration for this and sign up sooner rather than later.

BUCKET RANK:

Taking a vacation with former and current Steelers players is a dream for Black and Gold fans who don't get seasick, and Leadership League in Pittsburgh provides that opportunity.

Leadership League handles all commercial travel for the Steelers and also manages Tunch Ilkin's speaking engagements and social media endeavors. When Ilkin brought up the idea of starting a Steelers cruise, Leadership League was a natural to put it together.

The first one launched in 2014 and fans and current and former Steelers such as Antonio Brown, Franco Harris, James Harrison, Greg Lloyd, Dermontti Dawson, and Donnie Shell, to name a few, sailed to the Bahamas.

"A lot of people do it as a gift or an anniversary or the celebration of a special birthday," Leadership League co-owner Anne Williams said. "The players are very interactive with the fans and you bump into them everywhere you go. They're dining with them, they're swimming with them, they're playing basketball with them."

There are events too that bring together the Steelers and fans such as viewings of past Super Bowls in a theater and talent shows that have featured Hines Ward dancing (go figure), J.T. Thomas playing the piano, and Chris Hoke performing the "Hokey Pokey" with his kids.

In addition, extras can be purchased on the cruise such as a private dinner with one of the Steelers or a workout with players such as Brown and Harrison. A workout with Brown and/or Harrison has to come with this caveat: these are two of the hardest workers in Steelers history and they may only know one speed. If you opt to work out with one of them be prepared to pass out or not be able to walk real well if at all the next day—or both.

"It's definitely a fun thing," Williams said of the cruise, not grinding through a workout with Brown or Harrison. "A lot of the passengers are displaced Pittsburghers or people who just follow the team and this is the vacation of a lifetime."

Attend the Steelers' NFL Draft Party

WHERE: Heinz Field in Pittsburgh, Pennsylvania

WHEN: The Saturday of every draft, so the end of April or the beginning of May

HOW TO DO IT: This is another event that the Steelers host so go to www.steelers.com or call (412) 697–7713 to register.

COST FACTOR: $$–$$$. It's peanuts to get into party and money spent all depends on how much of a weekend participants want to make of it.

DIFFICULTY FACTOR: ▮. Heinz Field has a lot of room.

BUCKET RANK: 🗑🗑🗑

The NFL draft is reality TV at its best. It captures the elation of players realizing a dream, the crushing disappointment of ballyhooed prospects who agonizingly wait to hear their names called, and it is impossible to script. The mock drafts that precede the selection process are proof of that; even those who make their living analyzing the draft are doing cartwheels if they bat .333 on their projected first-round picks.

The NFL has adroitly built the draft into a made-for-TV event—a prime-time one, no less—creating a common misperception about the event. Many fans think New York—or whatever other city has ponied up the cash needed to host the selection extravaganza—is where all of the action happens.

The truth is the team representatives at the draft are mere window dressing, far from where the decision making is happening. The Steelers' brain trust, for example, huddles in a room at team headquarters for three days calling in the picks from there following discussion and sometimes spirited debate.

The Steelers, like every other NFL team, are extremely guarded when it comes to the draft—and their true intentions preceding it. But they also make it inclusive for fans by hosting Steelers Fan Blitz on the third and final day of the draft. The event provides plenty of return for a nominal fee ($15 for adults and young adults and $5 for kids 12 and under).

The Steelers allow fans on the field at Heinz Field for the only time of the year and scores of current and former players attend the event to

THE PATH MIKE DITKA ALMOST TOOK

When former Steelers running back Dick Hoak received his roommate list from Penn State in 1957 it had him bunking with Mike Ditka. That is how close the two came to teaming up for the Nittany Lions.

Hoak, who starred at Jeannette High School, and Ditka, an Aliquippa standout, visited Penn State together and each verbally committed to Nittany Lions coach Rip Engle. Pitt, however, had enough time to convince Ditka to stay closer to home, and he and Hoak ended up playing against each other in college and the NFL.

Ditka, a Pro Football Hall of Famer, remains one of the most celebrated players and colorful characters ever to come out of Western Pennsylvania. He and Tom Flores are the only people to have won NFL titles as players, assistant coaches, and head coaches.

sign autographs. Skills sessions for kids ages 6–14 are held on one half of the field and fans can attempt field goals on the other half of the field.

One of the newest additions to the day is having fans, selected through Steelers Nation Unite, announce the team draft picks to the crowd at Heinz Field.

"We get people that come from halfway across the country," marketing manager John Simpson said.

EXTRA POINTS

The Steelers' Connection to Joe Montana

Mark Gorscak has been a Steelers scout for two decades and his position in high school might have prepared him for a position that requires a lot of grunt but vital work. Gorscak played center at Ringgold High School in Donora in the mid-1970s and spent his junior season snapping to a young quarterback with a flair for dramatics named Joe Montana.

Gorscak did not make it to the Pro Football Hall of Fame like his celebrated teammate but he distinguished himself as a player, coach, and scout. Gorscak was inducted into the Mid-Mon Valley Sports Hall of Fame in 2010.

Go to a High School Game to Appreciate Why Football Is Such a Part of Western Pennsylvania's Fabric

WHERE: Western Pennsylvania

WHEN: Friday nights starting in late August or early September and running through the first part of December

HOW TO DO IT: There are so many great places to watch a game but definitely go on a Friday night.

COST FACTOR: $-$$. Needing only a couple of bucks to watch a football game. What a quaint concept.

DIFFICULTY FACTOR: ▌. Most high school games don't sell out.

BUCKET RANK: 🗑🗑🗑

Sundays—and occasionally Monday and Thursday nights—may belong to the Steelers. Friday nights, however, are still the domain of high school football. Kids who make endless laps around the field in the time-honored teenage social ritual now do so checking cell phones. But the tableau of high school football remains largely the same despite the stampede of technology. This is especially true in Western Pennsylvania, where games still draw communities together in stadiums that offer bright lights without the TV timeouts and personal seat license requirements.

Western Pennsylvania has always embraced a working-class sensibility—and Pittsburgh has its reputation as a shot-and-a-beer type of city. Hence the love affair with football, and that passion starts at the high school level in large part because of the great players and teams the region has produced.

Johnny Unitas, George Blanda, Joe Namath, Joe Montana, Dan Marino, and Jim Kelly headline the future NFL passers who played in Western Pennsylvania, earning it the moniker "Cradle of Quarterbacks." Mike Ditka, Bill Cowher, and Mike McCarthy are among the Super Bowl–winning head coaches who hail from Western Pennsylvania and represent a small fraction of coaches who have enjoyed success at football's highest level.

Central Catholic High School is a perennial power that gave birth to Marino's legend. Aliquippa also has a long history of success, a thread that runs from Ditka in the 1950s to Darrelle Revis in the 2000s, despite the economic devastation—and resulting population drain—that hit the city when the steel mills closed in the 1980s. And Clairton reeled off a state-record 66 consecutive victories from 2009 to 2013, establishing a new benchmark of success.

Then there is Woodland Hills, which did not even come into existence until the end of the Ronald Reagan era. Despite its relatively young age, Woodland Hills is consistently among the schools with the most graduates in the NFL and it led the league in 2010 with six. Included on that list were Steelers safety Ryan Mundy, Dolphins defensive end Jason Taylor, Cardinals wide receiver Steve Breaston, 49ers cornerback Shawntae Spencer, Dolphins fullback Lousaka Polite, and Patriots tight end Rob Gronkowski.

Yes, before Gronk was Gronk he played his senior season at Woodland Hills after moving into the school district. Gronk landed at Woodland Hills for the same reason that many college recruiters don't need a GPS or Siri to find their way to the school, which is just outside of

Pittsburgh. Longtime coach George Novak has built Woodland Hills, which opened in 1987, into a powerhouse and pipeline for colleges and the NFL.

In late October of 2015, Novak's Wolverines were undefeated, ranked the No. 1 Quad-A team in the state and preparing for a showdown with conference rival Mount Lebanon at the "The Wolverena."

The stadium is wedged into a residential area of Turtle Creek, a working-class town with close proximity to the various communities that feed into Woodland Hills, and it can be an intimidating venue.

The bleachers on the home side of The Wolverena climb to the heavens and they are filled with fans who view winning as much of an autumn rite as the colors changing on the cluster of trees that tower over the stadium. October 23 was no different even though Mount Lebanon entered the game with an unbeaten record like Woodland Hills.

A perfect day on the penultimate week of the regular season gave way to a brisk night, and by the time the game pitting two regional powers against one another kicked off the air was as crisp as the popcorn that sells for $1.50 a bag at The Wolverena.

The Blue Devils struggled to contain Woodland Hills' supremely talented running back tandem, which merely put the Blue Devils in good company as well as a 21–3 deficit.

Miles Sanders, one of the top backs in the state, has the look—and the game—to fulfill predictions that he is the next star to come out of Woodland Hills. Sanders, who signed with Penn State in February of 2016, is blessed with speed and a powerful base that is the signature of good backs.

The 6', 205-pounder makes it look easy too, whether he is taking handoffs, running the wildcat as a quarterback or supplying hits and tight coverage as a cornerback. Jo-El Shaw is a 6'1", 227-pound sledgehammer who signed with Syracuse and, like Sanders, is also worth the price of admission ($5 at The Wolverena).

Each broke free for a long touchdown run to stake the Wolverines to a big lead but the Blue Devils staged a furious fourth-quarter rally. Just when it looked like Mount Lebanon would complete a shocking comeback, senior cornerback Tyriq Thompson caught a deflected pass in the end zone and raced all the way to the other end of the field. Penalties wiped out the score but not the game-saving interception and Woodland Hills survived the upset bid in a 21–16 win.

The level of play, the grit showed by both teams, and the atmosphere highlighted what makes high school football in Western Pennsylvania so enduring.

And $20 covered admission, parking, a burger, a bag of popcorn, and a hot chocolate with a couple of bucks to spare. It's hard to get more value for your dollar and it's like that at scores of stadiums in the Pittsburgh area where Friday night lights still mean something timeless.

The Steelers' Connection to High School Football

The Rooneys have never lost sight of why football is so ingrained in Western Pennsylvania. They are big supporters of high school football and allow the Western Pennsylvania Interscholastic Athletic Association to stage its championship games at Heinz Field every year.

That commitment puts a lot of stress on a playing surface that has already endured three months of Pitt and Steelers games.

But the Rooneys recognize how special it is for kids to play at an NFL stadium and the Steelers also regularly shoot footage of high school football during the season and show clips from games on their website.

Cardinal Wuerl North Catholic stands out among high schools in the Pittsburgh area in regards to its connection to the Steelers.

Dan Rooney starred at quarterback at North Catholic in the 1940s, and it is also the alma mater of general manager Kevin Colbert.

Then there is the present.

Former Steelers outside linebacker Jason Gildon entered 2016 in his second season as North Catholic's head coach. In his first season he coached his son as well as the sons of Mike Tomlin and Joey Porter, both of whom were freshmen in 2015.

The presence of Tomlin and Porter, the driving force behind the Steelers' 2005 Super Bowl run, does not create a spectacle as fans are generally respectful of them.

"People leave them alone and I think that's what they want," North Catholic athletics director Mike Burrell said. "They just want to be a dad on Friday night."

And Gildon just wants to coach though it is hard to imagine anyone having a higher profile among his peers because of what he did during an 11-year NFL career.

Gildon made three Pro Bowls in the 10 seasons he spent in Pittsburgh. His 77 sacks for the Steelers are still the most by any player in franchise history.

Gildon helped burnish the Steelers' pass-rushing reputation when they were known as "Blitzburgh" and he is part of the chain of outside linebackers that seemingly came off an assembly line.

Greg Lloyd and Kevin Greene preceded Gildon. Porter and James Harrison followed him. All of them tormented quarterbacks at what became the glamour position on the Steelers' defense.

Gildon, Harrison, Porter, and Lloyd combined for 265 sacks for the Steelers. Greene, who signed with Pittsburgh in 1992, led the team in sacks all three seasons he spent with the Steelers.

Gildon played primarily on special teams his first two seasons in Pittsburgh. When the Steelers turned him loose after not re-signing Greene he had extra motivation to play well.

"I didn't want to let [Lloyd and Greene] down and I think when Joey got here as a young guy I was able to convey that same message to him," Gildon said. "You take pride in being a linebacker for the Pittsburgh Steelers and when you get out there on the field your ability to go out and make plays not only represent yourself but the guys who came before you at that position."

Gildon could have never envisioned that he would become so entrenched in Pittsburgh after the Steelers selected the Oklahoma State product in the third round of the 1994 draft.

Before arriving in Pittsburgh, Gildon had heard of Franco Harris and the Steel Curtain. He also knew about Rocky Bleier from watching the TV movie *Fighting Back*, which chronicled Bleier overcoming incredible odds to establish himself as Harris' backfield mate in the 1970s.

That constituted the extent of Gildon's Steelers knowledge before starting a slow climb to the top of the organization's all-time sacks list and continuing his life in Pittsburgh.

Gildon is trying to make his mark as a coach while also trying to make football as safe as possible for his players. Gildon did not allow his sons to play organized football until they were in fifth grade and he is a stickler for fundamentals.

"That's part of the game that's been lost, technique and the proper ways to tackle and just the proper ways to play the game without so much involvement of the head," Gildon said. "The effort has to be made at the youth level. I think we're really going to have to look at, is it really beneficial for kids to play football, third, fourth grade, before you turn a certain age."

Gildon is in a unique position of coaching a player whose father happens to be an NFL head coach. But, he said, Tomlin has been nothing but supportive and gave "sound advice" when Gildon asked him about making the transition from position coach to head coach.

Gildon is serious about pursuing a career in coaching—and staying close to the sport that has already given him so much.

"I'm very passionate about the game," Gildon said, "and any time I can have an opportunity to give back the knowledge I've acquired I relish the opportunity."

Watch a Game at a Steelers Bar

WHERE: This can be done all over the country; Steelers bars can also be found outside of the United States.

WHEN: The NFL season

HOW TO DO IT: If you are looking for a Steelers bar simply type in those words as well as the area you are looking for them into Google. More often than not it will return plenty of options.

COST FACTOR: $$-$$$. It's going to cost a little bit to watch a game in a bar if you are eating and drinking.

DIFFICULTY FACTOR: ▐. Steelers bars are *everywhere*.

BUCKET RANK: 🗑🗑🗑🗑

Steelers bars symbolize the team's popularity and give Black and Gold fans outside of Western Pennsylvania a chance to gather for games, wave Terrible Towels and often indulge in foods and drinks that are from Pittsburgh.

Pierogis and Iron City, anyone?

It only makes sense that Steelers Nation has a strong presence in our nation's capital, and The Tortoise & Hare Bar and Grille is one of the premier Steelers bars in the Washington, D.C., area. Located just across the George Washington Bridge in Arlington, Virginia, it draws hundreds of Steelers fans for games.

"It's like three deep at the bar and the patio is packed," said Jeremy Hill, a manager at The Tortoise & Hare. "It's loud as hell in here."

Indeed, it isn't exactly a wine and cheese crowd that gathers for games. Steelers fans are so loud that some of the waitresses wear ear plugs, Hill said, and the decibel level is tied to some degree to the sale of I.C. Light, which is $3 a can.

Kielbasa and pierogis are also sold as well as Pittsburgh sandwiches, which are a knockoff of Primanti's sandwiches.

The Tortoise & Hare's rise as a Steelers bar is an unlikely one. It had been a Minnesota Vikings bar but those games only drew a handful of fans so management agreed to a switch when some regulars suggested it become a Steelers bar.

Its reputation is now such that Ed Tomlin, the older brother of Mike Tomlin, has been known to stop in for Steelers games. And The Tortoise & Hare maintains a Pittsburgh presence throughout the year.

I.C. Light, which requires special trips for the bar to purchase, is served year-round for Pittsburghers who have transplanted to the Washington, D.C., area. There is also Steelers and Pirates paraphernalia throughout the bar and restaurant.

The front patio, meanwhile, sports a banner that reads, "You're in Steelers Country"—and leaves no doubt to fans of other NFL teams that they will have to go elsewhere to watch their respective teams.

"We love it and it's been getting better and better every year," said Hill, a New Hampshire native who roots for the Patriots but also likes the Steelers. "All of us know that Steelers fans are hard core. There's a reason why it's called Steelers Nation."

Steelers Nation is strong in the heartland, and it is especially vibrant about a mile from famed Wrigley Field.

Al Vento, flanked by his brothers, helped found "Franco's Italian Army." The color which that fan club and its ilk added to the Steelers in the 1970s helped earn them a national following. Steelers bars all over the county and even the world are an expression of that vast following.

Chicago is just a flat-out fun city, and watching a Steelers game at Durkin's Tavern is an experience for fans, including the regulars who have been reserving the same bar stool or seat for years.

The place is legit—Durkin's has a framed proclamation from the city of Pittsburgh that confers Steelers bar status on it—and it doesn't quit. The Steelers polka song is played after every Pittsburgh touchdown while Terrible Towels wave and confetti dances in the air.

Imagine that scene when 300 or so Steelers fans are packed into Durkin's. That happens regularly, making it challenging for the servers to navigate as they deliver Iron City and I.C. Light among other beers to thirsty patrons.

"It's a fun crowd," Durkin's general manager Erin Fey said. "I love them."

Fey, a native Chicagoan, shows that love by reserving all but a couple of the 30 TVs in Durkin's for the Steelers even if the Bears are playing at the same time.

"I allow one TV per room for the Bears game," said Fey, who is a lifelong Chicago fan but now roots for the Steelers as well. "Maybe, if people are willing to give up a TV, I'll throw (another) game on too."

Nikki Kemerer lives in Chicago but grew up in Western Pennsylvania and is a die-hard Steelers fan. It never fazes her when she encounters Steelers fans in Chicago or just about anywhere when she travels.

The notable exception came in 2012 when Kemerer was living in Rome and stumbled upon a connection to her roots halfway across the world.

"I'm walking down this little side street and I see one of these big banners that says 'You're in Steelers Country,'" Kemerer said.

Yep, welcome to La Botticella, the most famous Steelers bar outside of the United States and as much of a must-stop for Black and Gold fans visiting Rome as the Colosseum.

Owner Giovanni Poggi leaves little doubt about his affection for Pittsburgh—and the Steelers in particular—with the décor. Walls are covered with Steelers jerseys as well as paraphernalia from other Pittsburgh sports teams and even colleges.

The signature Pittsburgh piece inside of La Botticella is a statue of Jesus wearing a Steelers helmet.

Poggi has earned a measure of Steelers fame with his bar and he has been a guest of the organization when he has visited Pittsburgh.

Tom Diecks owns Greater Pittsburgh Travel and he always recommends La Botticella to clients when they visit Italy. Diecks has been there several times and bought Steelers shirts with Italian writing on them.

La Botticella shows Steelers games on a projector screen as well as other sporting events from the United States. Diecks said he once watched a Rutgers-West Virginia football game at La Botticella.

"It's an interesting bar," he said, "and Pittsburghers love it."

Kemerer agreed.

"It would be like any bar in Pittsburgh but in Rome," she said.

Make the Steelers a Part of Your Wedding

WHERE: Heinz Field is available for wedding receptions, but incorporating the Steelers into a wedding can be done anywhere.

WHEN: Anytime

HOW TO DO IT: Call (412) 697-7740 to check on availability; otherwise brainstorm with your significant other about Steelers themes.

COST FACTOR: $$–$$$$. A reception at Heinz Field is going to be a significant cost.

DIFFICULTY FACTOR: █ If you plan ahead you should be able to reserve Heinz Field for a reception.

BUCKET RANK: 🗑🗑

No one is more of an authority in the union of weddings and the Steelers than Jen Detore.

The Greensburg, Pennsylvania, resident owns Fabulous Affairs, which handles chair covers, linens, and decorations for special events and Detore has worked a number of so-called Steelers weddings.

She had one in which the chair covers were black and gold with Terrible Towels commemorating the nuptials at every table setting. Place cards for table settings were in the likeness of Steelers jerseys and the bride and groom were so serious about the wedding theme that they made a gate for the entrance to DiSalvo's Station Restaurant in Latrobe to replicate the gate the players pass through on the way to the field for home games.

Even all of that, though, could not compare with the Detores' wedding on August 15, 2009.

Not that she or her husband, Mike, planned on taking pictures on Chuck Noll Field during a training camp practice, chatting up Steelers kicker Jeff Reed, and conducting interviews for Pittsburgh TV stations.

The Detores and Dave Briga and Sadie Roberts, the best man and maid of honor, respectively, had stopped at St. Vincent College on the way to the wedding reception with the hopes of taking pictures with the Steelers in the background.

They were posing far from the action of practice when Steelers director of security Jack Kearney pulled up in a golf cart.

They thought they were in trouble when Kearney told them to get onto the cart. Instead he rode them down to the practice fields and told a Steelers staffer to treat them like VIPs. Kearney invited them to stay until practice ended and meet other players and coaches but they reluctantly declined because they did not want to delay dinner at the reception.

"We regret not staying all the time," Jen Detore said.

What made the experience only better, despite extreme heat and humidity, is the Detores had made the Steelers a part of their wedding even before the fortuitous stop at training camp.

They had beer mugs with Steelers logos instead of wine glasses at the reception. And Briga and Roberts entered the reception with Styx's "Renegade" playing.

Numerous publications wrote about the Detores', uh, detour on the way to the reception. And Pittsburgh TV stations ran the story through the weekend.

"We still have people that come up and remind us about it," Jen Detore said.

Pictures from the day as well as a framed copy of a story that ran in *Steelers Digest* hang in their game room. Their daughter, Madelyn, offers further proof of their devotion to the Steelers.

The Detores were watching a preseason Steelers game when she was less than a year old and they said "touchdown" so much that she blurted it out as well at one point.

It was her first word.

Chapter 4

Learn How the Steelers Became the Steelers

Visit the Pro Football Hall of Fame

WHERE: Canton, Ohio

WHEN: It is open year-round and the hours are 9:00 AM to 8:00 PM, Memorial Day through Labor Day and 9:00 AM to 5:00 PM the rest of the year. The Hall of Fame is closed on Thanksgiving and Christmas.

HOW TO DO IT: The HOF website (www.profootballhof.com) provides everything from ticket prices to lodging and dining options and is the best resource for planning a trip to Canton. Those who can't make it to the Hall of Fame can go to Google as an alternative. Videos of Steelers' Hall of Fame speeches are easily found on the Internet and worth watching.

COST FACTOR: $$-$$$$. A day trip to the Hall of Fame won't set you back much, provided your credit card doesn't get too much of a workout at the gift shop. Admission ranges from $17 to $24 and season passes are sold as well. The cost rises significantly if you have to fly and then spend a couple of days in Canton, whether attending the HOF induction ceremony in August or making a vacation out of the visit to one of football's holiest sites.

DIFFICULTY FACTOR: ▮. The only caveat here is that going to the Hall of Fame can be a challenge if you want to attend the annual induction ceremony. The demand for hotels increases exponentially for the weekend that is a celebration of the NFL's past and the return of a new season. It takes planning and patience—and a few bucks—to visit the Hall of Fame during its biggest weekend of the year. But it is well worth it if one of your favorite players is getting enshrined in Canton.

🪣🪣🪣🪣🪣. The Steelers' imprint is all over the Hall of Fame, putting a trip to Canton high on the bucket list, especially for an induction ceremony. The speeches are always heartfelt, usually emotional and are the can't-miss part of the weekend. The magnitude of receiving a gold jacket is palpable during those speeches as former Steelers running back Jerome Bettis can attest. "That was a culmination and my opportunity to thank all of the people that had helped to get me to the point where I was," Bettis said of his 2015 induction. "There were some nervous moments beforehand but once I got up there I felt really comfortable."

• •

We have covered many of the bucket-list items but a big-ticket one is still out there, and it pulls together the best of the Steelers' history. The Pro Football Hall of Fame leads off this chapter, one that covers the Steelers' illustrious past and the recent period in which the team played in three Super Bowls and won two of them over a six-season span. The 1970s—and how an organization that had been an afterthought built a dynasty—dominates Steelers history but doesn't have an exclusive hold on it. This chapter jumps around but it is chock full of information and anecdotes that help tell the story of the Steelers.

The six Super Bowl trophies that the Steelers display at team headquarters aren't just a powerful symbol of their glorious past. They are also a not-so-subtle reminder to everyone in the organization of what is expected in the future.

Greatness—or at least the pursuit of it—may permeate the Steelers' practice facility but nowhere is it better encapsulated than in Canton, Ohio.

The city that is only about 100 miles west of Pittsburgh is home to the Pro Football Hall of Fame, a contained village that displays bronzed busts of all who have achieved football immortality. Canton tells their stories as well of those of the NFL.

It is not an exaggeration to say the Steelers have erected their own wing at the Hall of Fame and the HOF lists 27 inductees with significant ties to the Steelers.

That number doesn't include Dick LeBeau, who was a Hall of Fame cornerback for the Detroit Lions, but coached 11 seasons for the Steelers and burnished his reputation as an innovator while serving two stints as the team's defensive coordinator. It also doesn't include Tony Dungy, who got the call to the Hall in 2016 as a coach but played two seasons for the Steelers, later worked for Noll, and considers Chuck Noll his greatest coaching influence.

Steelers started pouring into the Hall of Fame shortly after the great players from the 1970s started retiring. That and Pittsburgh's proximity to Canton regularly turned induction ceremonies into Terrible Towel–waving events.

That won't stop anytime soon as players from the 2005–10 Steelers teams that played in three Super Bowls become eligible for the Hall of Fame (more on those a little later).

A handful of former Steelers, meanwhile, could gain entrance to the Hall of Fame as senior candidates. The Hall of Fame Senior Committee nominates former players, coaches, and contributors who might have been overlooked for enshrinement.

The three Steelers who top that list for me are Art Rooney Jr., Donnie Shell, and L.C. Greenwood.

All were finalists for the Hall of Fame before dropping off the ballot and all might have encountered some silly if tacit rule about not letting too many Steelers from the 1970s into Canton.

Rooney quarterbacked the drafts that laid the foundation for the Steelers' dominance in the 1970s. Shell helped the Steelers win four Super Bowls and later made the NFL All-Pro team three consecutive

THE STEELERS LIST 24 OF THEIR OWN AS INDUCTEES INTO THE PRO FOOTBALL HALL OF FAME

Bert Bell, co-owner, 1963

John "Blood" McNally, coach/player, 1963

Art Rooney, founder, 1964

Bill Dudley, running back, 1966

Walt Kiesling, coach/player, 1966

Bobby Layne, quarterback, 1967

Ernie Stautner, defensive tackle, 1969

Joe Greene, defensive tackle, 1987

John Henry Johnson, running back, 1987

Jack Ham, linebacker, 1988

Mel Blount, cornerback, 1989

Terry Bradshaw, quarterback, 1989

Franco Harris, running back, 1990

Jack Lambert, linebacker, 1990

Chuck Noll, coach, 1993

Mike Webster, center, 1997

Dan Rooney, chairman and president, 2000

Lynn Swann, wide receiver, 2001

John Stallworth, wide receiver, 2002

Rod Woodson, cornerback, 2009

Jack Butler, cornerback, 2012

Dermontti Dawson, center, 2012

Jerome Bettis, running back, 2015

Kevin Greene, linebacker, 2016

Chuck Noll Saw Greatness in Kevin Greene

Kevin Greene, who made the Pro Football Hall of Fame in 2016 in his fifth year as a finalist, recorded 35.5 sacks from 1993 to '95 with the Steelers, and he once received the ultimate compliment from Chuck Noll. The former coach receded into retirement following the 1991 season, largely steering clear of the Steelers so he wouldn't cast a shadow over his successor, Bill Cowher. But he attended a game at Three Rivers Stadium when Greene was playing for the Steelers and he took notice of him. "I was sitting next to Chuck watching the game and very early on he said, 'Boy that 91's pretty good,'" said former Steelers director of communications Joe Gordon. "That coming from Chuck Noll that quickly...after that I was a big Kevin Greene fan."

seasons in the early 1980s. Greenwood was a charter member of the Steel Curtain and the Steelers credit the six-time Pro Bowler with 68.5 career sacks, third-most in team history.

Greenwood will likely get into the Hall of Fame one day—Joe Greene has said it is a football injustice that Greenwood does not yet have a bust in Canton—but he won't get to experience it as he passed away in 2013 at the age of 67.

Shell will get a Hall of Fame bounce from Dungy, who picked his former Steelers teammate to present him at the 2016 induction ceremony. That visibility should at least generate conversation about Shell, whose 51 interceptions still rank third on the Steelers' all-time list behind Hall of Famers Mel Blount and Jack Butler.

Rooney's drafts from 1970 to '74 are the stuff of legend, but will Hall of Fame voters allow a third Rooney into Canton? His father, Art, and brother, Dan, are already Hall of Famers, and if Art Jr. is going to join them he will need the Senior Committee to nominate him.

Of more immediate Steelers links to the Hall of Fame, Alan Faneca advanced to the final 15 in the 2016 voting and it is only a matter of when the former guard makes it to Canton. Here are four other Steelers who are still playing or recently retired who at least merit strong consideration for the Hall of Fame in the coming years.

S Troy Polamalu: The eight-time Pro Bowler is a likely first-ballot Hall of Famer. Polamalu (who is eligible for the Hall in 2020) and Ed Reed are the two best safeties of their generation. The criteria for a Hall of Famer is elastic and personal preference is also a factor, but Polamalu checks off every box.

QB Ben Roethlisberger: Big Ben is a lock, in my opinion, even if he never throws another pass. He has won a pair of Super Bowls and played in three of them. He owns every major passing record in Steelers history and if quarterbacks are ultimately judged by wins, consider this: Roethlisberger has never had a losing season and is one of only four quarterbacks to win at least 100 games in his first 150 starts. The others are Tom Brady, Joe Montana, and Terry Bradshaw.

WR Hines Ward: There is a bit of a logjam at wide receiver and Ward, who is eligible for the Hall of Fame in 2017, may have a wait as long as Jerome Bettis did—as deserving as he too is of football immortality. The trouble Ward might encounter is he was never considered an elite wideout and never fit the prototype of a dynamic pass catcher. But he is a Super Bowl MVP, finished his career as one of only nine NFL players with 1,000 career catches and is in the conversation for best blocking wide receiver of all time. He will get to Canton at some point.

OLB James Harrison: I believe Kurt Warner's incredible story— from bagging groceries, to playing in the the Arena Football League to achieving NFL greatness—should count when it comes to Hall of Fame consideration. Same goes for Harrison, who was cut four times by the Steelers before he finally stuck with them in 2004. His 75 career sacks after the 2015 season ranked second in Steelers history and no pass rusher played better than Harrison over a four- or five-season span, including 2008, when he won NFL Defensive Player of the Year honors.

Plays and Events That Shaped the Steelers— and Explain Their Six Lombardi Trophies

The "Immaculate Reception" is the greatest play in NFL history and it delivered the Steelers' first-ever playoff win.

Strip away the dramatic ending, the euphoria that ensued and the white-hot rivalry it created with the Raiders and it is fair to pose this question: Did the play fundamentally alter the Steelers' course of history?

The Steelers lost the following week in the AFC Championship Game to the Miami Dolphins, who then completed the only perfect season in NFL history by winning Super Bowl VII. The Raiders exacted a satisfying measure of revenge the following season when they drilled the Steelers 33–14 in the divisional round of the AFC playoffs.

It wasn't until 1974 that the Steelers broke through, winning at Oakland in the AFC Championship Game and then beating the Vikings in Super Bowl IX. That came after the draft that produced four future Pro Football Hall of Famers and remains the gold standard in the NFL (more on that draft later in this chapter).

That influx of talent put the Steelers over the top and led to the organization winning four Super Bowls from 1974 to '79. Sure, the "Immaculate Reception" provided a shot of confidence to a franchise that needed it, but the Steelers' course probably doesn't change if Franco Harris gets to the ball a fraction of a second later or if his catch

Santonio Holmes (10) is congratulated by his teammate Mewelde Moore after scoring a touchdown during the fourth quarter of Super Bowl XLIII against the Arizona Cardinals, Sunday, February 1, 2009, in Tampa, Florida. The Steelers won 27-23. (AP Photo/Gene J. Puskar)

is illegal because officials rule that teammate Frenchy Fuqua touched the ball first.

Something much more significant, in fact, happened three years earlier than the "Immaculate Reception" even if nobody knew it at the time. Such is the whim of history that a game between two teams in the midst of lousy seasons played a huge part in shaping the Steelers of the 1970s.

The Bears struggled for years to find a franchise quarterback after missing out on one because of a lost coin flip. The Steelers, meanwhile, don't own the '70s without Bradshaw.

. . . .

The Tackle That Saved the Steelers

B en Roethlisberger won two Super Bowls before he celebrated his 27th birthday and collaborated with Santonio Holmes on one of the greatest plays in the game's history. He has thrown for more than 40,000 yards and Roethlisberger became the first NFL quarterback to throw for 500 yards in two separate games.

For all that Big Ben has done to have has right arm bronzed, it is his legs that provided arguably his most significant play in Steelers' history.

It came in the 2005 playoffs when the Steelers were on the verge of finishing off the Colts and pulling off a stunning upset in Indianapolis. The Steelers held a 21-18 lead with one minute, 20 seconds left in the game when Roethlisberger handed off to Jerome Bettis at the 1-yard line.

Bettis bounced right as he tried to score the game-clinching touchdown but lost the ball after a jarring hit by Colts linebacker Gary Brackett.

The ball bounced to cornerback Nick Harper at the 7-yard line, and he was off to the races with the Steelers in goal-line personnel (i.e., big bodies and no wide receivers on the field).

"I laid out for my block and I just remember turning around in the pile and seeing everybody taking off running in the wrong direction," recalled former Steelers guard Alan Faneca, "and just going 'Oh nooo. What the hell is going on?'"

The stunning turn of events had Roethlisberger running backwards, trying to keep Harper in front of him so he could get a good angle for a tackle attempt.

"It was just so unbelievable when it happened," Roethlisberger told me in 2014, "and it was just find a way to make a play."

He did, at around the Colts' 40-yard line, when Roethlisberger got enough of Harper's right foot to get him to the ground. The Colts, however, still had more than a minute left in the game and Peyton Manning drove them to inside the Steelers' 30-yard line.

Rookie cornerback Bryant McFadden broke up a pass in the end zone, a play that would loom as large as the one Roethlisberger had made after Bettis' fumble. That forced a 46-yard field goal attempt by Mike Vanderjagt, one of the best kickers in the game—and one of the most confident.

"Coach [Bill] Cowher calls the timeout and Vanderjagt looks over at him like, 'Yeah, what's that going to do?' And then he shanks it," former Steelers defensive Brett Keisel said. "Kickers are built to have confidence and that was his way of showing confidence like, 'I've got this, your timeout's not going to do anything.'"

The most egregious miss of Vanderjagt's career allowed the Steelers to escape with a white-knuckle victory and they went on to win the Super Bowl for the first time since 1979.

"If I make that play and we lose the game no one's talking about it," Roethlisberger told me almost a decade later. "But because we won the game it became such a big deal."

As it should have.

The Steelers had suffered so many near-misses under Cowher—they lost three AFC Championship Games at home from 1997 to 2004—that blowing that game in Indianapolis would have been utterly devastating.

Would they have won two Super Bowls and played in three of them from 2005 to 2010 if they lost to the Colts in the most heartbreaking of scenarios? We'll never know thanks to Roethlisberger's tackle coupled with Vanderjagt's shank.

"Maybe this little so-called dynasty doesn't start if Ben doesn't make that tackle," said former Steelers quarterback and Roethlisberger understudy Charlie Batch.

James Harrison's Remarkable Rise to Stardom

Another key pivot in Steelers history rated as a mere footnote when it happened—and even that might be generous.

An injury that outside linebacker Clark Haggans sustained while lifting weights during the off-season carried over to training camp. Needing a body at outside linebacker, the Steelers signed James Harrison, who had already been cut three times by the organization.

Harrison, who had also been cut by the Ravens before a fourth stint with the Steelers, has said that he would have pursued another career had he not stuck with the team that year.

Not that Bill Cowher had any interest in hanging on to Harrison.

Harrison, who initially signed with the organization in 2002 as an undrafted free agent, struggled with the complexity of NFL defenses and sometimes let his frustration over not getting more of a look get the better of him. That could be misconstrued and lead to questions about whether he could be coached by those who were trying to mold Harrison into an NFL player.

"He was hard-headed but that's to be expected from young guys coming in," said former Steelers outside linebacker Jason Gildon, who played for the team from 1994 to 2003. "I think James' problem early on was establishing that rapport with the coaches. You almost ask yourself, 'Well, why [learn] if I'm not going to play?' It was a maturity thing and I think as time went on he realized that's part of being a professional."

Harrison's return to the Steelers in 2004 would have been short-lived had Dick LeBeau not returned to the organization as well that season.

LeBeau came back as the Steelers' defensive coordinator—he held the same position in 1995–96—after three seasons as the Bengals' head coach and then a season as an assistant head coach to good friend Dick Jauron in Buffalo.

LeBeau saw something in Harrison even though the latter struggled with a new defense. When Cowher wanted to release Harrison after Haggans got healthy LeBeau talked him out of it.

He told Cowher he would take responsibility for teaching Harrison the defense and that the Steelers would regret it if they let him get away.

Harrison made enough progress to stick with the team. He developed into a valuable special-teams player while biding his time as a reserve outside linebacker over the next couple of seasons.

The Steelers released Joey Porter in 2007 in large part because they had seen enough from Harrison to believe he was ready to start and give them a much less expensive option at right outside linebacker.

Harrison staged his coming-out party that season in a nationally televised win over the Ravens. Harrison recorded three and a half sacks, forced three fumbles and intercepted a pass in the Steelers' 38–7 romp, and that performance helped propel him to the first of five consecutive Pro Bowls.

Harrison has since won the NFL Defensive Player of the Year Award, retired at Steelers' headquarters, and then saved the Steelers in what has been a splendid second act after injuries depleted them at outside linebackers in 2014.

Harrison's 75 sacks with the Steelers were the second most in franchise history at the end of the 2015 season, his second one since coming out of retirement. He returned for presumably his final NFL season in 2016 at the age of 38, and in addition to giving the Steelers a solid pass rusher Harrison has become a mentor in the locker room.

A prickly persona early in his career would have made that seem unlikely for the player his teammates had nicknamed "Deebo," after the bully in the movie *Friday*.

But Harrison has an unbelievable work ethic and, as he has shown with his career, anything is possible when it to comes to him.

Harrison has never forgotten what LeBeau did for him and the two are extremely close. When LeBeau got inducted into the Western Pennsylvania Sports Hall of Fame, Harrison flew into Pittsburgh to surprise him. When the Steelers did not renew LeBeau's contract in 2015, Harrison told his former mentor he would join him in Tennessee if he said the word.

LeBeau, who took a job as assistant head coach with the Titans, told Harrison to do what was best for his family, so Harrison stayed in Pittsburgh, where he will finish his career.

That Harrison would have switched teams less than two months shy of his 37th birthday shows how loyal he is to LeBeau, and for good reason. Who knows what would have happened with Harrison had LeBeau not talked Cowher out of cutting him in 2004?

The Steelers history would be a little different—and they certainly wouldn't be able to lay claim to the play LeBeau has called the greatest in Super Bowl history.

Going the Distance in Super Bowl XLIII

I covered Troy Polamalu for almost 10 seasons and I never once saw him snap at a reporter. He was always polite even if he frequently did not have much more to say than "God willing" in response to any number of queries.

But when Polamalu felt like talking he could be pure gold. That turned out to be the case after an off-season practice in 2014 when I asked him about Harrison's 100-yard interception return for a touchdown in Super Bowl XLIII.

Polamalu warmed up to the subject right away and he revealed how close that play came to not happening with the Arizona Cardinals at the Steelers' 2-yard line right before halftime.

The Cardinals were poised to at least tie the score at 10 heading into intermission when the teams lined up with less than 20 seconds left in the second quarter. Polamalu anticipated from the formation that Cardinals quarterback Kurt Warner would throw a slant pass to wide receiver Anquan Boldin.

The problem for Polamalu, who rarely hesitated to follow his instincts, is that he was on the other side of the field. As he pondered switching sides, Polamalu concluded that the initial hesitation had cost him too much time and he stayed put.

Good thing for the Steelers that he did.

Harrison feigned a blitz, took one step back and ran right in front of Boldin. Had Polamalu raced over and also tried to jump the route, the eight-time Pro Bowler told me, there is a good chance he would have run into Harrison. That would have given the Cardinals an easy touchdown or at worst an incomplete pass with two more cracks to score a touchdown—and you can't like those odds with a quarterback who had completed 11 of 12 passes for five touchdowns inside opponents' 20-yard line in the postseason prior to Harrison's pick.

What Harrison did after the interception truly made the play a once-in-a-generation one. Harrison followed a convoy of blockers down the right side of the field, dodging Cardinals tacklers before collapsing in the opposite end zone while carrying two Arizona players.

The return looked a little disjointed at first, with cornerback Deshea Townsend all but trying to take the ball from Harrison. But the blocking that ensued after Harrison shooed Townsend away was anything but random.

LeBeau had instilled in his players the importance of turning defense into offense following a turnover. If defensive players didn't find someone to block after a fumble recovery or interception, even in practice, LeBeau didn't hesitate to "blast" them.

"We were all held accountable and when you go through film if you're not doing your job you address the situation, so that's what being put on blast is," former Steelers defensive end Brett Keisel said. "It was something we worked on all the time."

That work paid off on football's biggest stage and Harrison's interception return for a touchdown proved to be the difference in the Steelers' 27–23 win over the Cardinals.

"Everyone wants to look Santonio's catch as winning a Super Bowl but James' play was a 14-point turnaround," Polamalu told me in reference to Santonio Holmes' toe-tapping touchdown catch at the end of the game. "It won us a Super Bowl. It's the second-greatest play in Steelers history."

And the greatest in Super Bowl history.

. . . .

A Look at the Pre-1970s Steelers

The Steelers might not have won consistently before Chuck Noll arrived and the Rooney sons, particularly Dan and Art Jr., established prominent voices within the organization. But fans, especially younger ones, would be mistaken to think that the Steelers' history starts in the 1970s, when they launched a dynasty and propelled themselves to national popularity.

The Steelers had their share of great players before ones like Mean Joe and Franco and Bradshaw.

For decades, Ernie Stautner, a tougher-than-leather defensive tackle, was the only Steelers player to have his number officially retired. And Stautner is one of a handful of Steelers players from the pre-1970s who is in the Pro Football Hall of Fame.

That list includes Bobby Layne, a transcendent quarterback who played hard on and off the field. The Steelers have a fascinating history with quarterbacks (more on that later in this chapter) and Layne is part of that.

The Steelers traded for the Texas gunslinger in 1958 after he had helped the Detroit Lions win two NFL championships. He played five seasons for the Steelers and made two Pro Bowls but never led them to the playoffs.

He took a liking to the young running back out of Penn State and Dick Hoak can't explain why to this day. The two ran in different circles, with Hoak commuting to work and returning each night to his wife, while Layne lived in a hotel—and lived the single life with bachelors and players who did not bring their families to Pittsburgh for the season because they couldn't afford it.

Hoak would establish himself as one of the Steelers' better players in the '60s—he is still sixth on the team's all-time rushing list—and he found out one night that Layne didn't just want him close by on the field.

The Steelers were playing an exhibition game on the road and Hoak encountered a group of teammates playing cards and drinking when he wandered into the hotel lobby. Layne spotted Hoak and asked him to sit beside him for good luck. Hoak obliged until it got to be around 2:00 AM and he left the group and went to bed.

"The next morning we had an early meeting and I was tired and [Layne] walked in there and it looked like he had [gotten] 12 hours of sleep," Hoak recalled with a laugh. "It was like he was never even out the night before. That's what he could do."

Layne, who died in 1986 at the age of 59, had said his biggest regret in football was not delivering a championship to Art Rooney. The final season he played for the Steelers before retiring did leave a significant legacy.

The Steelers won a franchise-best nine games in 1962, against five losses. Their success coincided with a decision by Dan Rooney to put the Steelers' logo on just the right side of the team helmets. When longtime equipment manager Jack Hart asked Rooney after the

BLACK AND GOLD
IN THE HEARTLAND

The Steelers share their practice facility and Heinz Field with Pitt. They share a uniform scheme with a school hundreds of miles away from the 412 area code and their connection to the University of Iowa dates back to the late 1970s.

The Hawkeyes had gone almost two decades without a winning season when Hayden Fry took over as head coach for the 1979 season. Fry put his psychology degree to use as soon as he arrived in Iowa City and he quickly turned his attention to the Steelers as he tried to change the culture of a once-proud program.

"Hayden's deal was [the Steelers'] jersey signified winning and that's what we want to get to," longtime Iowa football equipment manager Greg Morris said.

Morris worked as a student athletic trainer in Fry's first season at Iowa but he still remembers vividly how the colorful coach wanted to replicate the Steelers' uniform—and how cooperative the Steelers were after receiving the request.

The Steelers, Morris said, sent a full uniform complete with a No. 12 jersey, which had been made famous by quarterback Terry Bradshaw. Iowa copied the uniforms, from the helmet and jersey sleeve stripes all the way down to the socks.

That wouldn't happen today with all of the licensing issues that would be in play. But Iowa ran with the black and gold motif with the Steelers' blessings, and in 1981, Fry's third season, they returned to the Rose Bowl for the first time since 1958.

Fry, who also famously had the walls in the visiting locker room painted pink to curb aggression, led Iowa to three Rose Bowls and 11 other bowl appearances in 20 seasons and was named Big Ten Coach of the Year three times. He was inducted into the College Football Hall of Fame in 2003.

season if he wanted stickers put on both sides of the helmet, Rooney said no because of the Steelers' success that season.

The Steelers have maintained that tradition, giving their helmets a unique look, and they built on their success in 1963. They entered the final week of that season with a 7–3–3 record and needing a win over the Giants at Yankee Stadium to advance to the NFL Championship Game against the Bears.

The Steelers knew they could play with anyone that season, including George Halas' mighty Bears. The Steelers had tied the Bears 17–17 earlier in the season in a game they probably should have won. Hoak scored what would have been a key touchdown on a pass reception after dragging several Bears tacklers into the end zone.

But officials ruled that Hoak's forward progress had been stopped; the Bears kicked a late field goal to escape Forbes Field with a tie.

"It was a bad call," Hoak said. "If we had won that game we probably would have won a championship too."

The Steelers lost to the Giants—a team they had earlier beaten 31–0—missing a trip to the championship by a game. The Steelers proceeded to go in reverse after 1963 and won just 18 games over the next five seasons.

But that period led to the coaching change that transformed the organization.

Charles Henry Noll, though only 38 years old when the Steelers hired him, wasted little time taking charge of the team.

Shortly after he arrived in Pittsburgh, he called Andy Russell over to his office. Russell had just made his first Pro Bowl and he figured Noll wanted to congratulate him. His first meeting with his new coach turned into a dousing with a cold bucket of water.

"He said, 'Russell, I've been watching the game films and I don't like the way you play. You're too out of control. You're too aggressive,'" Russell recalled. "I was like, 'Whoa!' Nobody ever told me I was too aggressive."

His teammates received similar treatment when Noll made his first speech at training camp that year. He told the Steelers that they had been losing because they weren't any good. He also told the players in the room that he planned to get rid of most of them.

"I think," Russell said, "that five of us from that room made it to the [first] Super Bowl."

A new era had begun.

The Greatness of Chuck Noll

Noll and Bill Cowher and Mike Tomlin, who followed Cowher, all fit the profile of young, thirty-something assistant coaches on the rise. Each had his own approach but all proved they were capable of leading a team—and commanding respect even from players not much younger than they were.

If the hiring of Noll established a template for an organization that had cycled through head coaches for too long, Noll himself established a standard that remains unmatched.

He and Bill Belichick are the only coaches to win four Super Bowls; Noll is the only coach in NFL history to win all four Super Bowls in which his teams played.

He harnessed the talent that the Steelers stockpiled with a direct, no-frills style and a demeanor that could come across as detached if not aloof. His real genius, however, was his eye for detail and his meticulous approach to the game.

Noll, above all, was a teacher and he enjoyed the process as much as the wins that came in his 23-year coaching career.

"Let's say you blocked the wrong man. When you're coming off the field you can see that stern look that coach Noll used to have. Instead of him telling you, 'You screwed up!' His first question to you was 'What were you thinking?'" former Steelers running back Frenchy Fuqua said. "When I did make a mistake and was corrected in that manner it made me think, *Frenchy, were you thinking when you walked up to the line?* I think it made us a better team mentally and he would even do that in the meetings while we were watching film. And I never wanted to be put in that situation, what were you thinking? I always called him a student-of-the-game coach."

Noll, in truth, was a student of life.

He got his pilot's license and became a wine connoisseur and his desire to be well-rounded hardly stopped there. Noll could talk about almost any subject, something that made him an excellent party host, and the only reason the public didn't see more of his personality is Noll never wanted it to be about him.

He turned down all kinds of endorsement opportunities, preferring they go to his players. After he stunned Dan Rooney on December 26, 1991, by telling the Steelers president he was retiring Noll quickly receded into the background.

He held a position with the team after that but it was largely ceremonial until Noll's death at the age of 82 on June 13, 2014.

No one in the Steelers organization knew Noll better than Joe Gordon.

The two joined the Steelers in 1969 and Gordon served as the team's communications director during Noll's tenure. What is revealing about Noll—and a trait he never lost even when his health started to fail him—is a story Gordon often tells when asked about his enduring memories of the man.

Prior to a Steelers AFC Championship Game against the Oilers, Noll stopped in Gordon's office and saw a broken shelf on top of a cabinet. Noll proceeded to fix it, totally immersed in the task despite the magnitude of the game that started in just a couple of hours.

"This was typical of him," Gordon said.

That love of fixing things and tinkering with gadgets made Noll the repair man of choice for Steelers broadcaster Myron Cope.

The colorful Cope had dubbed Noll "The Emperor" because he reigned supreme as a coach and the two lived one near one another in the Sewickley section of Pittsburgh. They taped a regular show in Cope's basement and Noll often gladly put in a little overtime after the two had finished.

Size Never an Issue with Jack Ham

Jack Ham's size had been enough of a concern coming out of high school that he received Penn State's last scholarship after another player turned it down. Art Rooney Jr., who headed the Steelers' player personnel department when the team drafted Ham in the second round in 1971, saw why questions about Ham's size lingered even after he became a two-time All-American at Penn State. The Steelers were hosting players they had drafted at a Pittsburgh hotel and when Ham knocked on the door to Rooney's room, Rooney asked Ham if he was delivering a letter. The reason: he mistook Ham for a bellhop because of his size. Ham added 15 pounds of muscle once he got to the NFL and proved to be plenty big enough during a 12-year career with the Steelers. He made eight consecutive Pro Bowls and his interception in the 1974 AFC Championship Game proved to be a turning point in the Steelers' 24–13 win at Oakland. Ham made the Pro Football Hall of Fame in 1988, his first year of eligibility for it.

"Any time there was any little problem in the house, if a screen door was unhinged or some other minor problem in the household, Myron's wife, Mildred, would say 'You've got to get that fixed,'" Gordon recalled. "He'd say, 'No, Chuck's coming over on Sunday morning. He'll fix it.'"

One of Noll's best repair jobs came near the end of his career.

The team started 0–2 in 1989, losing by the combined score of 92–10 to the Browns and Bengals. That followed a 5–11 season in 1988 and the national media descended on Pittsburgh, including NBC's O.J. Simpson.

The inevitable stories about whether the game had finally passed Noll by did not rattle the Steelers. Noll simply called the team together and told his players to stay the course because what they were doing worked.

The Steelers beat the favored Vikings 27–14 that Sunday at Three Rivers Stadium and went 8–5 the rest of the season. They returned to the playoffs for the first time since 1974 and upset the Oilers 26–23 in the wild-card round.

SUCCESS OUTSIDE PITTSBURGH

Here are three Steelers draft choices who never played for the team but found success away from the NFL:

Ara Parseghian, 13th round in 1947: The Miami (Ohio) product played two seasons for the Browns, who also drafted him in 1947, before a hip injury cut short his career and put him on a path to Notre Dame lore. Parseghian became head coach of the Irish in 1974 and led the team to a pair of national championships in 11 seasons. Parseghian was inducted into the College Football Hall of Fame in 1990.

Gene Keady, 19th round in 1958: A three-sport star at Kansas State, Keady went into coaching instead of pursuing a playing career and is one of the most successful coaches in Big Ten men's basketball history. Keady won conference coach of the year honors seven times from 1980 to 2005 at Purdue. He retired with a career record of 493–270.

Tom Jurich, 10th round in 1978: The longtime athletics director at Louisville kicked at Northern Arizona—and for one game for the New Orleans Saints—before embarking on a career in sports administration.

Only a dropped pass the following week in Denver prevented the Steelers from advancing to the AFC Championship Game. That season ranked up there with any as far as Noll's coaching jobs and the genius of the man always went back to one thing: Noll's ability to teach.

"I don't believe that I would have learned the game, learned about being an offensive lineman, learned about being a professional any other place like I learned here," said Tunch Ilkin, who played for Noll from 1980 to 1992. "One of the things he'd always say is "Understand what's going on here, understand what we're trying to do, understand what the people you're playing against are trying to do.' Playing for him, it wasn't enough just to know your position but to know what everybody understood on the offensive line and to understand conceptually what you were trying to accomplish

EXTRA POINTS

Mining the Mid-American Conference for Greatness

The Steelers made 584 draft choices from 1970—the year of the AFL-NFL merger—through 2016 and only 14—or roughly two percent—have come from Mid-American Conference schools. But to say the Steelers have done well when drafting from the MAC might be an understatement.

Quarterback Ben Roethlisberger, wide receiver Antonio Brown, and linebacker Jack Lambert all played in the conference that operates in the shadow of the Big Ten. Cornerback Ron Johnson, the Steelers' first-round pick in 1978, also hailed from a MAC school, and the Eastern Michigan product started 62 games and intercepted 13 passes in seven seasons with the Steelers.

The Steelers' history of drafting players from off-the-radar schools is well-documented. The organization has, however, stuck mostly to schools from the college football establishment since coach Mike Tomlin and general manager Kevin Colbert joined forces in 2007. The Steelers made 83 picks from 2007 to 2016 and 68 of those came from the five power conference schools or Notre Dame. Six hailed from Big Ten powerhouse Ohio State, including first-round selections Cameron Heyward (2011) and Ryan Shazier (2014).

offensively and to understand conceptually what the defense was trying to do that you were playing against. He would stop practice and say this all of the time, 'Understand what we're trying to do here,' and everybody would take notice."

Fuqua paid his former coach the ultimate compliment when he said the older he got the smarter Noll became.

"A lot of the things he told us back then wound up being a whole lot more true as we matured and you realize what he was telling you," Fuqua said. "I love Chuck Noll. I would run through a damn brickhouse for him."

Building a Dynasty

The Steelers' drafts after the arrival of Noll in 1969 turned into the stuff of legend. Writers have waxed poetic about those drafts for decades, making it oh so fitting that the first draft choice in franchise history was a Notre Dame back by the name of Bill Shakespeare.

Yep, the Steelers took Shakespeare, the so-called "Bard of South Bend," with their first-round pick in 1936 when they were still the Pittsburgh Pirates. Shakespeare never signed with Pittsburgh, instead opting for a career in business where he could make considerably more money.

Steelers drafts through their first three-plus decades did not produce much more than interesting tidbits such as the name of their first-ever pick. And by the mid–1950s the draft had become an afterthought to an organization that struggled to find a winning formula.

In 1959 and 1963 the Steelers traded their first seven picks. Those drafts bookended ones in which the Steelers dealt five of their first six picks for four consecutive years. The Steelers' apparent disdain for the draft can be traced to the dynamics of the organization at the time. Buddy Parker had little patience for rookies—and the mistakes they inevitably made because of their youth—and owner Art Rooney refrained from telling the head coach how to do his job.

Dan and Art Rooney Jr. were too young to challenge their father's longstanding policy when it came to the head coach or the organization's approach to the draft and the Steelers traded 20 more picks from 1964 to '68.

Everything changed when the Steelers hired Noll in 1969. He was much closer in age to the Rooney brothers and his belief dovetailed with theirs that making the draft a top priority offered the best way to build a team and achieve the long-term success that had eluded the Steelers.

In 1969, the third and final year that the NFL and AFL held a joint draft—the leagues merged in 1970—the Buffalo Bills took running back O.J. Simpson with the No. 1 pick. The Atlanta Falcons followed with the selection of Notre Dame offensive tackle George Kunz, and the Philadelphia Eagles took Purdue running back Leroy Keyes.

The Steelers held the No. 4 pick and a consensus had crystallized around a defensive tackle from North Texas State with seemingly superhuman strength.

"We agreed on Joe Greene and that really started the thing right," Art Rooney Jr. said.

Just as significant as the selection of Greene, who had been harder to block at North Texas State than the sun, was the foundation that the Steelers had put into place before drafting him.

The Steelers started rating draft-eligible players by position and assembled a list of the top 100 to 150 players regardless of position. The rankings were compiled from reports filed throughout the year as well as meetings between the coaches and scouts leading up to the draft. The Steelers vowed to stay true to their draft board and only use need for a position as a tiebreaker if they were trying to decide between two players who had similar rankings.

That system—and the Steelers' commitment to building through the draft—still prevails within the organization. The early success the Steelers had with it shows why it has endured.

Noll's first draft landed Greene, offensive lineman Jon Kolb, who became a mainstay at left tackle, and defensive end L.C. Greenwood.

The next year the Steelers took quarterback Terry Bradshaw with the first overall pick and stole cornerback Mel Blount in the third round.

Fans pour into Heinz Field prior to the Steelers' final home in 2015. Scenes such as these can be traced to the 1970s, when the Steelers won four Super Bowls and their popularity exploded.

He developed into a ferocious and iconic middle linebacker and is one of the reasons why the Steelers' draft in 1974 is the best in NFL history and will likely never be surpassed. The Steelers drafted eventual Pro Football Hall of Famers with four of their first five selections, including Lambert and Webster. They also landed the pieces that allowed them to put everything together and win four Super Bowls from 1974 to '79.

"The stars were lined up on that, weren't they?" Rooney Jr. said.

Were they ever.

It started in the first round, where the Steelers had to wait 20 selections before making their first pick.

Noll loved a wide receiver from Alabama A&M named John Stallworth. The scouts preferred Lynn Swann, an acrobatic wideout from UCLA. Swann, however, did not run all that well during testing, raising concerns since he wasn't the biggest guy.

Swann agreed to run the 40-yard dash right before the draft for BLESTO scout and former Steelers great Jack Butler. He clocked in at under 4.6 seconds, allaying concerns about his speed and the Steelers took Swann in the first round.

They were between Lambert and another linebacker in the second round. Defensive coordinator Woody Widenhofer broke the tie when he said both players would need time to learn the defense but that Lambert could help immediately on special teams.

The Steelers, incredibly enough, did not have a third-round pick the year they aced the draft. Even more astounding: Stallworth was still available (more on that later) when the Steelers made the first of two picks in the fourth round and No. 82 overall.

One reason Stallworth had slipped so far is that when he had a chance to compete on a big stage at the Senior Bowl, the coaches played him as a defensive back. The Steelers pounced on the player they had considered drafting in the first round and then took cornerback Jimmy Allen with their second selection of that round.

They completed their haul in the fifth round when they drafted Webster, an undersized but strong player from Wisconsin. Webster had jumped out to the Steelers when they were watching film of a Big Ten defensive tackle they really liked.

Webster dominated him and after playing behind Ray Mansfield early in his career, he became the hub of the Steelers' offensive line and arguably the greatest center in football history.

An Equation That Explains the Steelers' History with Quarterbacks

Quarterback is the most important position in all of sports, as the Steelers' history can attest. The franchise won four Super Bowls with Terry Bradshaw but did not capture the elusive one for the thumb until 25 years and 13 different starting quarterbacks after winning it all in 1979.

Nothing better sums up the Steelers' star-crossed history at the position than this equation: JC+DR−DM=BR. Its origins trace back to the spring of 1983 when Bradshaw was nearing retirement and, in fact, had just eight NFL passes left in his right arm. The Steelers were in a position to take his successor in the 1983 NFL draft, ballyhooed for its quarterbacks, especially after Dan Marino started to free fall.

Marino was already a Pittsburgh legend at that point, having starred at Central Catholic and then Pitt. A senior season that did not match the brilliance of his junior campaign, when Marino led the country with 34 touchdown passes and finished fourth in Heisman Trophy balloting, resulted in five quarterbacks getting drafted ahead of him.

The Steelers, in hindsight, should have sprinted their first pick to the podium at New York Sheraton Hotel with Marino still available at No. 21 overall. And they might have, had team president Dan Rooney not been so honest. Rooney, as he recalled in his eponymous autobiography, bumped into *Pittsburgh Press* sportswriter John Clayton at Three Rivers Stadium before the Steelers made their first pick. Clayton, now with ESPN, told Rooney that the Steelers should trade quarterback Cliff Stoudt for a second-round pick and use their first selection on Marino. Rooney loved the idea. So did Chuck Noll, Art Rooney Jr., and Dick Haley—until they asked how he had come up with it.

When Rooney told them the truth they waved him off. The Steelers taking draft advice from a sportswriter? Yeah, right. They instead drafted Texas Tech defensive tackle Gabe Rivera, whose career ended tragically his rookie season when a car accident left him paralyzed from the waist down. "We could have drafted Marino, and I believe if we had we would have won more Super Bowls in the 1980s," Rooney wrote in *Dan Rooney: My 75 Years With The Pittsburgh Steelers and The NFL.*

Memories of what could have been led Rooney to be proactive two decades later when the Steelers found themselves at another critical juncture involving a quarterback. The Steelers were coming off a 6–10 season and picking 11th overall in the 2004 draft. Eli Manning and Philip Rivers went first and fourth—and were promptly swapped in a trade between the Giants and Chargers. That caused the Steelers to turn their focus to Arkansas offensive tackle Shawn Andrews a season after they had averaged just 3.3 yards per carry, still their lowest in a season since the 1970 NFL-AFL merger.

The Steelers were intrigued by Ben Roethlisberger, who had the size and arm that NFL teams covet, but not the polish of Manning and Rivers after starting just two seasons at Miami (Ohio). When final discussions started on whom the Steelers should take first in the draft Rooney said in his book that he helped "steer" the conversation to Roethlisberger. The Steelers ending up taking Roethlisberger over Andrews, a selection that proved to be a crucial for an organization that had played in just one Super Bowl since the 1970s.

What might have been after Clayton broached Rooney with his Marino idea played a significant part in the Steelers drafting Roethlisberger. Hence, the aforementioned equation.

The intrigue when it comes to quarterbacks and the Steelers goes back a lot farther than Roethlisberger and Marino.

ANOTHER QB WHO SHINED AFTER GETTING OVERLOOKED BY THE STEELERS

Johnny Unitas isn't the only Pro Football Hall of Fame quarterback that the Steelers let get away. Two years after drafting Unitas, the Steelers took Purdue star Len Dawson with the fifth overall pick of the 1957 NFL draft. He didn't play much as a rookie and became expendable when the Steelers traded for Bobby Layne, another future Hall of Famer, in 1958. They dealt Dawson to the Browns after the 1959 season—he threw just 17 career passes for the Steelers—but he didn't become a star until he signed with the Dallas Texans of the AFL in 1962. Dawson emerged as one of the game's top quarterbacks in Dallas and became a legend in Kansas City after the team relocated there and changed its nickname to the Chiefs. He won MVP honors in Super Bowl IV after leading Kansas City to a 23–7 upset of Minnesota.

The Steelers selected a flat-topped quarterback by the name of Johnny Unitas in the ninth round of the 1955 draft after Rooney pushed for it even though the team had a glut of quarterbacks. Rooney knew Unitas—or at least his game—well. The two had been star high school quarterbacks at the same time and Unitas had, in fact, beaten out Rooney for a spot on the Pittsburgh's All-Catholic League first team in 1950. Rooney had always been intrigued with Unitas and he correctly surmised that the Steelers stole him in the draft following a productive career at Louisville.

Unitas never got much of a look from the Steelers in his only training camp with the team in large part because of coach Walt Kiesling.

Kiesling favored veterans over rookies and he scoffed at Unitas' slight stature and also questioned whether he had the smarts to run an NFL offense. Kiesling's stance left Dan Rooney in a delicate situation. He considered Kiesling a mentor who taught him more than anyone about the game at the pro level. He was also only 23 years old at the time the Steelers drafted Unitas, adding to the difficulty of challenging the well-established Kiesling. But Rooney and his four brothers, particularly Tim, felt so strongly about Unitas that they lobbied on his behalf to their father. The elder Rooney refused to undercut his head coach and the Steelers released Unitas after their final preseason game in 1955.

Unitas spent a year playing semi-pro football for a Pittsburgh team and working at a steel mill. A letter-writing campaign that Unitas started in hopes of getting a legitimate shot in the NFL finally paid off when the Baltimore Colts signed him as a backup. An injury to Colts starter George Shaw early in the 1956 season provided the only opening Unitas would need. He proceeded to author an epic career in which he made 10 Pro Bowls, won four NFL MVP Awards, and led the Colts to a world championship in 1958 and a Super Bowl title in 1971.

The 1958 overtime win over the Giants came in a nationally televised game and put pro football on a course to becoming a billion-dollar industry as well as the most popular sport in America. "In my mind, he's by far the greatest quarterback in football history," Rooney wrote in his autobiography.

. . . .

Bill Cowher and the Steelers' Return to the Top

The surprise retirement of Chuck Noll came at a critical juncture for the Steelers. The sheen from the four Super Bowl titles in the 1970s had faded, and from 1980 to 1991 the Steelers won just two division titles and did not advance past the divisional round of the playoffs.

The Steelers' search for Noll's successor led them no further than their backyard in one sense. They hired Bill Cowher, who had grown up in nearby Crafton and at age 34 became the youngest head coach in the NFL.

Cowher coached like he had played as a special-teamer with the Browns and Eagles: intense and all over the place like the spittle that sometimes flew from his mouth. He wore his emotions as if they were a part of his wardrobe, and with a chin that looked like it had been forged in a Pittsburgh steel mill he proved to be a perfect fit for the Steelers.

"We had one-on-one drills in practice and he was getting fired up and he was out there running sprints with us," recalled former Steelers center Dermontti Dawson, who played four seasons for Noll before Cowher took over as head coach. "He was right in the mix with everything we did as players and it was more interactive, a total contrast."

Tunch Ilkin, the Steelers' starting left tackle when Cowher was hired, had played against Cowher and was the same age as his new coach. Ilkin loved playing for Noll but he quickly embraced Cowher too because of the contrast.

"He wasn't trying to be like Chuck or anybody else. He was just himself. I think that's why it worked," Ilkin said. "Bill was a terrific coach and I thought that was great that he wasn't influenced by that. I thought it was really great that when Chuck retired he kind of stepped back and he wasn't sticking around to be a help. He allowed that transition to go smoothly."

It went better than that.

Cowher joined Paul Brown as the only NFL coaches to lead a team to the playoffs in their first six seasons. The Steelers returned to the Super Bowl in 1995 and played in three AFC Championship Games from 1994 to '97.

They weathered some lean seasons under Cowher but in 2004 the Steelers won 15 consecutive games with rookie Ben Roethlisberger playing quarterback after losing their season opener.

The season, however, ended with a crushing loss to the Patriots at Heinz Field, dropping the Steelers to 1–4 in AFC Championship games under Cowher.

The next season the Steelers won seven of their first nine games but then dropped three in a row to fall to 7–5 heading into the final month of the regular season. With little to no room for error the Steelers reeled off four consecutive wins.

Jerome Bettis punctuated the first of those victories by running over Bears linebacker Brian Urlacher in a 21–9 win at snowy Heinz Field. That play served as a fitting metaphor for the rest of the regular season as the Steelers trampled their final four opponents by a combined score of 115–33.

If it seemed like they were sailing that wasn't an accident. Cowher started a theme with his players when it looked like they might miss the playoffs, telling them to imagine they were on the water with nothing else around to distract them.

"The basic scene was the same," former Steelers guard Alan Faneca said. "We were on a ship for six weeks and were hearing stories about us on a ship for 20 to 30 minutes of this team meeting and he would weave it around football terms to us and what was happening that week and things to do on a ship. It's you and the sea and nothing else and you don't worry about anything else."

The Longest Run

Speed, scheme, and exquisite execution resulted in the touchdown run that helped the Steelers win their fifth Super Bowl. "Fast" Willie Parker broke off a 75-yard run on the second play of the third quarter after flashing through a huge hole at Ford Field. Guard Kendall Simmons and tackle Max Starks crashed in the right side of the line and guard Alan Faneca wiped out Seahawks linebacker Lofa Tatupu after pulling from the left.

Parker scored easily on the run that remains the longest in Super Bowl history. The Steelers had noticed that the Seahawks shifted their defense to the left when they anticipated a pass to the left side of the field. When the Steelers, leading 6–3, got the look they wanted quarterback Ben Roethlisberger changed the play from a pass to 34 Counter Pike. Parker's burst gave them a double-digit lead on the way to a 21–10 victory. "We were setting up that run the whole game," Faneca said.

The Steelers rode that message to NFL history.

They prevailed four times in the postseason, becoming the first No. 6 seed to win the Super Bowl. Their 21–10 victory over the Seahawks in Super Bowl XL wasn't a Picasso but it gave Bettis, whose teammates so badly wanted to win him a ring before he retired, the perfect ending to his career.

It added the missing piece needed to bridge the current teams with the ones that had won four Super Bowls in the 1970s. The victory also validated Cowher, a master motivator who had been at his best in leading the Steelers to their first world championship in 25 seasons.

"I tell people today one of the best things he did as a coach was every single week he put a mission in front of us and had the team focused for the rest of the week on that one mission, whatever it was he thought we needed to do to for that week to beat that opponent," Faneca said of Cowher, who resigned after the 2006 season and has since worked as a studio analyst for CBS. "He did that week in and week out and sometimes it wasn't much and sometimes it was a lot. But when you left that first team meeting on Wednesday morning, everybody was working toward the same goal and it got everybody going towards the game."

Mike Tomlin and a Sixth Super Bowl Title

The question came as the Steelers prepared for Super Bowl XLIII in Pittsburgh, after media from all over the country had descended on their practice facility. Mike Tomlin was asked by a national NFL reporter about some of the Steelers players saying he had improved in his second season as a head coach.

Tomlin, unwilling to play along for a presumably feel-good story about his precociousness as a coach, retorted that it wasn't their job to judge him; it was his job to evaluate them.

Both the answer and the question were telling when it came to the man who succeeded Cowher. Tomlin's reaction revealed why he had been able to establish control of a veteran locker room from the outset. The question underscored how fraught with pitfalls the job was when Tomlin accepted it in January of 2007.

The Steelers were a year removed from winning the Super Bowl when Cowher stepped down after an 8–8 season. The core of the 2005 championship team had remained intact and the prevailing thought was that the Steelers would promote from within the organization.

They had two worthy in-house candidates in offensive coordinator Ken Whisenhunt and assistant head coach/offensive line coach Russ Grimm. Each made the list of four finalists along with Bears defensive coordinator Ron Rivera and Tomlin, who had been a defensive coordinator for a season with the Vikings, one in which they went 6–10.

Tomlin, after much speculation and some confusion, was hired over Grimm. At the age of 34 and with only eight seasons of NFL experience on his résumé, he became just the third Steelers head coach since 1969.

"Some guys wanted the Rooneys to promote from within. Some guys wanted Whisenhunt. Some guys wanted Russ Grimm," former Steelers quarterback Charlie Batch said. "But it got to that point where when the Rooneys decided, everybody said, 'There's a reason why they've only had two coaches [since 1969]. If they selected him, we go with it.'"

It did not take long for a veteran-laden team to understand why the Rooneys had turned over one of the NFL's flagship franchises to someone young enough that he had played against Steelers linebacker and locker room leader James Farrior in college.

"The No. 1 thing he needed to do was command the attention," Batch said, "and he was able to get that in his very first meeting even though he was only two or three years older than some of the guys in that locker room. He was able to relate to guys and get the best out of them."

"You could tell he loved the game of football," said former Steelers defensive end Brett Keisel, who played five seasons for Cowher before Tomlin became head coach. "He knew about it, he loved studying it, he loved watching it. He's a great motivator and a great speaker. We knew we were in a situation where a lot of us had been together a long time and we had a great rapport together and just a great, great vibe in the locker room."

A CLOSER LOOK AT SANTONIO HOLMES' STEELERS LEGACY

Santonio Holmes made one of the greatest catches in Super Bowl history and his toe-tapping grab in a 27–23 win over the Cardinals in the 2008 Super Bowl delivered a sixth Lombardi Trophy to the Steelers.

Ironically enough, Holmes' missteps while with the Steelers led to his second-greatest contribution to the organization. The Steelers dealt the former Super Bowl MVP to the Jets in 2010 after Holmes became too much of a headache. The trade netted a fifth-round draft pick—the Steelers had drafted Holmes in the first round of the 2006 draft—and looked like a paltry return for an elite talent at wide receiver.

Now it is merely one of the best trades in franchise history.

The Steelers traded the pick they received from the Jets to the Arizona Cardinals during the 2010 NFL draft for cornerback Bryant McFadden and a sixth-round pick. They took Antonio Brown with that selection, No. 198 overall, and he is on his way to becoming the best wide receiver in franchise history. Brown has already won three Steelers MVP Awards, something accomplished by only three other players. And he is re-writing the Steelers' record book during a stretch that is among the best ever by an NFL wide receiver. Over 2014–15, Brown became the only player in NFL history with consecutive seasons of at least 120 catches and at least 1,600 receiving yards.

The Steelers won 10 regular-season games in Tomlin's first season as well as the AFC North. They ran out of gas—Tomlin ran such a physically demanding training camp that the Steelers may have lost their legs—and fell to the Jaguars in the divisional round of the 2007 playoffs.

The unwavering confidence Tomlin had in himself, however, helped set up a championship season in 2008.

First some background: Tomlin had broken into the NFL as a defensive backs coach with Tony Dungy, a Chuck Noll disciple, and Tampa Bay. He spent five seasons with the Buccaneers before becoming the Vikings' defensive coordinator in 2006. He spent one season with the Vikings before arriving in Pittsburgh, full of energy and charisma.

Tomlin had run a 4-3 defense in Minnesota and that, coupled with Dungy's influence, fueled nervous speculation after the Steelers hired him. The Steelers had long employed a 3-4 defense and fans fretted that he would make major changes to a team built for a 3-4—and built to win now.

A first-time head coach less secure with himself might well have insisted on making an imprint on the side of the ball that was his expertise. What did Tomlin do? He left the defense, at least schematically, alone and didn't meddle with what coordinator Dick LeBeau had been doing. He also retained many of Cowher's defensive assistants.

That continuity paid huge dividends in 2008.

A Steelers defense that was experienced but with most of its key players in their prime emerged as the top one in the NFL—as well as one for the ages (see the breakdown on the next page).

It carried an offense that dealt with line and injury issues all season as the Steelers won 12 games and defended their AFC North title.

THE 2008 DEFENSE STIRRED ECHOES OF THE STEEL CURTAIN

Shortly after the Steelers parted ways with longtime defensive coordinator Dick LeBeau in 2015, the city of Pittsburgh designated February as Dick LeBeau Month for that year. City Council also presented him with a key to the city in a ceremony attended by Steelers outside linebacker James Harrison and former Steelers defensive end Brett Keisel.

A humbled LeBeau talked extensively about the defense that might be nearest to his heart of all that he has coached and for good reason. The 2008 unit led the NFL in scoring (13.9 points allowed per game) and total defense (237.2 yards allowed per game) and keyed the Steelers' run to a sixth world championship.

"LeBeau talks about that year all the time and says that was an amazing year and that he doesn't think that will ever get beaten because of today's NFL," Keisel said.

The 2008 defense compares favorably with any in Steelers history, including the vaunted Steel Curtain units. It also stacks up with great ones in recent NFL history from a statistical standpoint. Here is a look at the 2008 defense in seven categories compared with six other great defenses, including three from the Steelers:

Yards per play	Yards per carry
1974 Steelers, 3.6	2000 Ravens, 2.7
1976 Steelers, 3.8	1976 Steelers, 3.2
2008 Steelers, 3.9	**2008 Steelers, 3.3**
1975 Steelers, 4.2	2015 Broncos, 3.3
2000 Ravens, 4.3	1974 Steelers, 3.4
1985 Bears, 4.4	1985 Bears, 3.7
2015 Broncos, 4.4	1975 Steelers, 4.2

Rushing yards per game
2000 Ravens, 60.6
2008 Steelers, 80.3
1985 Bears, 82.4
1976 Steelers, 104.1
1974 Steelers, 114.9
1975 Steelers, 130.4

Net passing yards per attempt
1974 Steelers, 4.3
1975 Steelers, 4.6
2008 Steelers, 4.7
1976 Steelers, 5.0
1985 Bears, 5.4
2015 Broncos, 5.6
2000 Ravens, 5.7

Net passing yards per game
1974 Steelers, 104.7
1975 Steelers, 131.1
1976 Steelers, 133.2
2008 Steelers, 156.9
2000 Ravens, 176.0
1985 Bears, 187.3
2015 Broncos, 199.6

Total yards per game
1974 Steelers, 219.6
2008 Steelers, 237.2
1976 Steelers, 237.3
1985 Bears, 247.9
2000 Ravens, 258.4
1975 Steelers, 261.5
2015 Broncos, 283.2

TDs allowed
*1976 Steelers, 14
1985 Bears, 16
*1975 Steelers, 17
2008 Steelers, 19
*1974 Steelers, 21
2000 Ravens, 22
2015 Broncos, 29

*14-game season

The one time the defense faltered in 2008, Roethlisberger and the offense picked it up.

After the Steelers allowed a pair of fourth-quarter touchdowns in Super Bowl XLIII to fall behind the upstart Cardinals, Roethlisberger led an eight-play, 78-yard drive. He and Santonio Holmes played pitch and catch all the way down the field in the last two minutes of the game and connected on a six-yard touchdown to deliver a 27–23 win.

The victory made Tomlin, at age 36, the youngest coach to win a Super Bowl. The Steelers returned to the Super Bowl two seasons later but couldn't summon any late-game magic in a 31–25 loss to the Packers.

The Steelers missed the playoffs in 2012 and 2013 but seem poised to make a run at the Super Bowl in the coming seasons after rebuilding their defense on the run. Tomlin has his critics because of his game management but after nine seasons as head coach his six playoff appearances tied Noll and Cowher for that many in the same span.

And his .639 winning percentage topped both Cowher (.597) and Noll (.591) after their first nine seasons. Tomlin has never had a losing season. Nor has he lost a team. That his voice still resonates in the Steelers' locker room—and the patience ownership has shown with head coaches dating back to Noll—bodes well for Tomlin staying with the Steelers for quite some time.

Chapter 5

From Baltimore and the AFC North to Hollywood

A multitude of bucket-list items have been detailed for you. The Steelers' rich history has also been covered. Now it is time to venture out to the rest of the NFL, from road trips to take to the significance of Steelers rivalries—present and past. There is no better place to start than in the AFC North, with a certain team that raises the temperature more than any other.

The Steelers and Baltimore Ravens don't agree on much. One could say up and the other would say down. Then they would roll up their sleeves and brawl over it.

The two AFC North rivals did find common ground on the official retirement of Joe Greene's No. 75 jersey in 2014.

Not that the Steelers consulted the Ravens about it after Greene requested they retire his jersey during the November 2 game against Baltimore at Heinz Field. But John Harbaugh was downright giddy after learning during a conference call with Pittsburgh reporters about Greene picking the Ravens game for his jersey ceremony.

"Did he really?" the Ravens coach said. "I will take that as an honor. Wow, that's something pretty special."

So is the Steelers-Ravens rivalry, and Greene picking their game to have his jersey retired affirmed that. The man literally traded punches (and kicks) with the Browns during his career. He played his last down more than a decade before the Ravens were born. Yet Greene knows that the Ravens are unquestionably the Steelers' biggest rival.

He is also well aware that anything that can provide an edge when the two meet, such as the féting of a legend, could very well swing the outcome.

Pittsburgh held a 24–20 advantage in the win-loss column after the 2015 season, but two losses to the Ravens in 2015, who only won three other games, nearly kept the Steelers out of the playoffs. The teams, meanwhile, have split their 36 games against one another since 2000; half of those have been decided by three points or less.

"It's a rivalry only when either team has the ability to win the game," former Steelers running back Jerome Bettis said. "That's what makes the rivalry, whenever we play we have no clue who's going to win the game and that's what makes it really special."

The Steelers and Ravens were already well-acquainted when the NFL returned to Baltimore in 1996. That is because Art Modell yanked the Browns out of Cleveland and moved them to Baltimore. Modell renamed his team the Ravens and they traded drab brown and orange colors for purple and black. But, said former Steelers outside linebacker Jason Gildon, "they were still at heart the Cleveland Browns."

It didn't take long for the Ravens to shed that label. They won the Super Bowl in their fifth season behind a dominating defense, and since 2002, when Jacksonville and Tennessee moved to the AFC South, they have been locked into a bitter struggle with the Steelers for supremacy in the AFC North.

The acrimony between the two teams, interestingly enough, can be traced to the similarity of the two organizations.

Each places a premium on stability as well as building through the NFL draft. Each organization also prides itself on playing a physical, blue-collar brand of football that embodies the ethos of its city.

Those systems collide when the Ravens and Steelers play, making those games organizational tests of soul. Add to that the stakes that are usually involved when the AFC North rivals meet and it is easy to see why this is as black and blue a rivalry as there is in all of sports.

The physical toll these games exact can be staggering.

Steelers rookie running back Rashard Mendenhall broke his shoulder blade less than a half into his first Ravens game in 2008. Five seasons later, Le'Veon Bell, another Steelers rookie running back, got knocked out while trying to score a late-game touchdown in Baltimore.

Steelers quarterback Ben Roethlisberger still says Ravens linebacker Bart Scott's sack in 2006 in Baltimore is the hardest hit he ever took. Two years later, Ryan Clark delivered arguably the hardest hit in a rivalry fueled by them when the Steelers safety leveled Ravens running back Willis McGahee at the end of the AFC Championship Game.

And when Scott threatened to kill wide receiver Hines Ward after a 2007 game it wasn't because the Steelers had clobbered the Ravens 38–7 on national TV. Scott was upset because Ward had blown up him and Ravens safety Ed Reed with blocks.

"Hines played the game the way strong safeties play the game," former Steelers guard Alan Faneca said. "Strong safeties get a lot of little cheap licks because they're not always accounted for, especially in the run game, but they get to come up and make a tackle albeit eight yards down the field. Hines kind of rubbed most teams wrong."

Faneca said the Ravens did the same to the Steelers.

"They loved to talk about it and talk about how good they were and we were a team that loved to show you how good we were and prove it on the field," said Faneca, who played in 21 Steelers-Ravens games. "They were big talkers. We were big doers."

Joey Porter didn't talk?

"Joey was a big talker too," Faneca said, "but we did it first."

The Ravens developed into such a rivalry during Faneca's time with the Steelers that he said they represented coach Bill Cowher's "two off weeks" during the season. Cowher was a master motivator but he didn't have to do anything to get his players up for the Ravens.

That has continued since Cowher left the Steelers after the 2006 season, and if anything the Ravens and Steelers have become more similar.

Each hired young head coaches within a year of one another, and Harbaugh and Mike Tomlin have each won a Super Bowl while elevating the NFL's best rivalry.

The Ravens hold a 10–9 series lead since Harbaugh and Tomlin became head coaches and 12 of those games have been decided by three points or less.

Tomlin is only 10–11 against Baltimore—he was a combined 29–8 against the Steelers' other two division rivals after his first nine seasons—but a list of his greatest wins would have a serious crab cakes flavor to it. A strong argument can be made, in fact, that Pittsburgh's five most memorable wins over Baltimore have come during Tomlin's tenure. Agree? Disagree? Here are my five in order of significance:

Steelers 23, Ravens 14; January 18, 2009: The AFC North rivals have only met once in the conference title game and the Steelers put away the Ravens with one of the most electrifying plays in franchise history. Troy Polamalu dropped into coverage after reading the eyes of Joe Flacco and he intercepted the rookie quarterback. He didn't stop there with the Steelers holding a tenuous 16–14 lead in the fourth quarter. Polamalu weaved his way 40 yards for a touchdown. Clark delivered the coup de grâce on the ensuing possession when he blasted McGahee with a shot so vicious that it knocked out both players.

Steelers 13, Ravens 10; December 5, 2010: Another one of Polamalu's signature moments came with Pittsburgh trailing 10–6 in a classic Steelers-Ravens street fight. The Ravens did not account for Polamalu on a third-down blitz midway through the fourth quarter and he sacked Flacco, forcing a fumble that LaMarr Woodley recovered on Baltimore's 9-yard line. Roethlisberger, playing with a broken nose, did the rest. He somehow dragged Terrell Suggs long enough to throw the ball away and avoid what would have been a killer sack on first down. Roethlisberger then threw a 9-yard touchdown pass to backup running back Isaac Redman on third down. The defense made the Steelers' only touchdown stand up and Pittsburgh wouldn't have won the AFC North—or make a run to the Super Bowl—if it hadn't beat Baltimore at M&T Bank Stadium.

Steelers 13, Ravens 9; December 14, 2008: The Steelers credit Roethlisberger with 39 career fourth-quarter comebacks. None this side of Super Bowl XLIII was finer than the masterpiece he put together with the Steelers trailing 9–6. Roethlisberger completed seven of 11 passes for 89 yards after the Steelers had taken possession at the Ravens' 8-yard line with just over three-and-a-half minutes left in the game. He capped a 12-play, 92-yard drive with a four-yard touchdown pass to Santonio Holmes that broke the goal line by mere inches, and the victory gave the Steelers a regular-season sweep of the Ravens for the first time since 2002. That proved to be the difference in the Steelers winning the AFC North—and the Ravens having to play at Heinz Field when the teams met a third time in late January.

Steelers 31, Ravens 24; January 15, 2011: The obituaries for the Steelers had started in the Heinz Field press box after the Ravens took a stunning 21–7 lead into halftime of an AFC divisional playoff game. But Clark—who loved to hit and talk and was built for Steelers-Ravens—forced a fumble and intercepted a pass in the third quarter. Both led to touchdowns. What stung the Ravens more: Roethlisberger completed a 58-yard pass on third-and-19 with just over two minutes left to play in a tied game. Antonio Brown, then a little-known rookie, secured the catch on the side of his helmet and the Tyree-esque grab led to the game-winning touchdown.

Steelers 23, Ravens 20; December 2, 2012: The Steelers trailed by 10 points in the first half and seven points in the fourth quarter against the eventual Super Bowl champions. That didn't stop backup quarterback Charlie Batch from rallying the Steelers in Baltimore a week after they had committed a ghastly eight turnovers in a loss to the Browns. This is the Steelers' most improbable victory over the Ravens, though the shine from it quickly faded. The Steelers lost their next three games to fall out of playoff contention.

A Steelers Haven in Baltimore

Steelers embassies in the form of bars can be found throughout the Baltimore area for transplanted Pittsburghers. One of the most well-known havens is Todd Conner's in Fells Point.

It is located right in the heart of Ravens country but defers to the Steelers when they are on TV even if that rankles some of the regulars.

"For a Steelers-Ravens games this is one of the hottest bars to be at," said Douglas Considine, a manager and bartender at Todd Conner's. "As a bartender, I'm part sociologist and it's one of the most fascinating things I've seen in my life. It's so insanely complicated."

Considine said games between the fierce AFC North rivals usually draw about 51 percent Steelers supporters and 49 percent Ravens fans. That makes for an interesting study and contrast between two fan bases that don't care for one another.

Todd Conner's is a solid alternative for Steelers fans if they don't have tickets to a game in Baltimore. Imagine half the bar going nuts when the Steelers make a big play and vice versa for the Ravens and it's a pretty intense scene.

The charged atmosphere can't match being at the game. But Todd Conner's gives those who are invested in arguably the best rivalry in the NFL a chance to experience the intensity of it.

Steelers-Browns

One of the NFL's oldest rivalries has also turned into one of its most lopsided ones. Nothing better reflected that than a conversation between Ben Roethlisberger and Landry Jones on the home sidelines near the end of another Steelers win over the Cleveland Browns.

Roethlisberger congratulated Jones on winning his first NFL start and both got a chuckle since the former did the heavy lifting in the Steelers' 30–9 win over the Browns on November 16, 2015, at Heinz Field.

A sprained ankle sent Jones to the sidelines early and Roethlisberger entered the game a week after spraining his foot in a win over the Oakland Raiders. All Roethlisberger did despite a bum wheel was throw for 286 yards in the first half on the way to a 379-yard, three-touchdown masterpiece.

"Maybe the most expensive backup in the NFL," Jones joked about Roethlisberger after the game.

Roethlisberger's showing reinforced how costly a decision the Browns made in 2004 when they passed on the native Ohioan in the draft and instead took Miami (Florida) tight end Kellen Winslow Jr. with the sixth overall pick. Roethlisberger is 19–2 against the Browns from 2004 to 2015 and has 20 victories against Cleveland if you count the one he delivered as Jones' "backup."

The pivot each franchise took in the 2004 draft has also defined a rivalry between two working-class cities that are separated by about 150 miles of turnpike. Since Roethlisberger's arrival the Steelers are 21–3 against the Browns and their average margin of victory during that span is 15.6 points, a staggering figure in a league that promotes parity.

The Browns, meanwhile, have made the playoffs just once since the NFL returned to Cleveland in 1999 because of a revolving door at quarterback. And who else but the Steelers beat them in a 2002 postseason game after the Browns squandered a 24–7 third-quarter lead?

The Browns are now on their ninth head coach since 1999 and even Bill Belichick couldn't win in Cleveland before former owner Art Modell moved the franchise to Baltimore. Adding to the sting of their string of futility to the Steelers: Their last five head coaches, prior to the 2016 hiring of Hue Jackson, have been fired following season-ending losses to Pittsburgh.

The Browns have had their moments against the Steelers, most notably in 2009. The Browns upset the Steelers 13–6 to drive a stake through Pittsburgh's hopes of defending its Super Bowl title.

The winds whipping off Lake Erie made for an even colder December night than usual in Cleveland, adding to the Steelers' misery after they bottomed out that season.

But games like that have been too few and far between for the Browns, diminishing the significance of the AFC's oldest rivalry and one that has been nothing if not manic.

Cleveland owned Pittsburgh prior to the Steelers' emergence in the 1970s. The Browns beat the Steelers 14 of 17 times from 1962 to 1970 and when Pittsburgh committed to building through the draft it did so because of the success of franchises such as Cleveland.

The Steelers dominated the '70s, winning 16 of 20 meetings against the Browns. Then the series settled into the one period of parity it has enjoyed.

The rivals played 33 times from 1980 to 1995, with the Steelers winning 17 games. Each team won 16 regular-season games against its rival during that span and 10 times the Browns and Steelers split the season series.

Former Steelers offensive lineman Tunch Ilkin played during that period, and he still has vivid memories of his first game at Cleveland's Municipal Stadium.

"The place just reeked of history," Ilkin said of the 1980 game. "Jim Brown and Paul Brown and all of the great players of the Browns. Not only did it reek of history but it reeked of urine because the plumbing in that facility was terrible."

Ilkin quickly learned that plumbing issues were the least of his concerns when Pittsburgh visited Cleveland.

He had played college ball at Indiana State and was not quite prepared for the raw hatred that came with the Steelers-Browns rivalry. When Ilkin went to take his helmet off during a break in pre-game warm-ups, veteran defensive end Dwight White told him to keep it on. Soon after that, Ilkin said, a battery went whizzing by his head. Another time, Ilkin said, a dog biscuit hit him in the head during a timeout. He looked around, seething, until fellow offensive lineman Craig Wolfley defused the situation.

"Wolf looks at me and goes, 'This isn't *Slap Shot*. What are you going to do? Climb into the stands and find the guy who hit you with a dog biscuit?' We all started laughing," Ilkin said. "They hated us. It was just this intense rivalry. It was nasty, guys fighting."

It had been that way before Ilkin joined the Steelers.

In 1976, Browns defensive tackle Joe "Turkey" Jones dumped Steelers quarterback Terry Bradshaw on his head, something that might earn a player a suspension if it happened today.

The year before, defensive tackle Joe Greene kicked center Bob McKay—and in the last place any man wants a cleat to connect— near the end of the Steelers' 42–6 win in Cleveland. Browns offensive lineman Tom DeLeone went after Greene and punches were thrown, leading to the ejection of DeLeone and Greene.

The two were later fined, as was McKay.

"They interviewed Joe maybe 15 years after and he went on to blame it on me and Dwight White," said former Browns offensive tackle Doug Dieken, who played for Cleveland from 1971 to 1984. "He said, 'I got so tired of listening to Dieken and Dwight scream at one another that I just lost it.'"

Dieken added with a laugh, "I told Joe, 'You've got a lot of guts blaming me for that.'"

Dieken, Cleveland through and through, is now color analyst for the Browns' radio broadcasts. He has gotten to know some of the players he once despised because of their Black and Gold attire and said the blood and guts that once defined Steelers-Browns are part of a bygone era.

"You hated them for that 60 minutes on Sunday," Dieken said. "But once you retired and got a chance to know them, hey, they were just like us except they got four more Super Bowl rings than we did."

Steelers-Bengals

This rivalry does not move the needle like Steelers-Ravens or have the proximity and history of Steelers-Browns. Heck, the Ravens quickly became one of the Steelers' biggest rivals because they were the Browns before Art Modell moved the team to Baltimore—and became less welcome in Cleveland than Terrible Towels.

So where does the Steelers-Bengals rivalry fit when assessing Pittsburgh's AFC North foes?

It doesn't label easily but there is no question the rivalry crackles like a raging fire. Nothing reinforced that more than when the teams met in Cincinnati in December of 2015.

The two teams nearly got into it during pre-game warm-ups at Paul Brown Stadium. On the first series of the game Steelers wide receiver Antonio Brown and Bengals cornerback Dre Kirkpatrick had to be separated after slapping at one another at the end of a play.

Pushing and shoving persisted throughout the contentious game and spilled over after the Steelers had beaten the Bengals 33–20.

Cincinnati left tackle Andrew Whitworth called out the NFL for not taking action against Vince Williams over a perceived threat the Steelers linebacker made against Bengals linebacker Vontaze Burfict after the rivals' first meeting of the season.

Steelers right tackle Marcus Gilbert took to Twitter to call out the Bengals for being all talk and state his hope that the teams would meet for a third time that season in the playoffs.

They did and what transpired during one of the wildest playoff wins in Steelers history made the contentious meeting between the rivals less than a month earlier seem like a pillow fight.

Consider that a Steelers *assistant* coach received an unsportsmanlike conduct penalty after getting into a shoving match with Bengals safety Reggie Nelson on Pittsburgh's sideline. The Mike Munchak–Nelson exchange had been reduced to a footnote by the end of the night because of what happened after the Steelers squandered a 15-point lead and then won 18–16 when rookie Chris Boswell kicked a 35-yard field goal in the waning seconds of the game.

Roethlisberger left the game at the end of the third quarter with a shoulder injury and Bengals fans rained down boos on him as he left the field for the Steelers' locker room. It looked like Roethlisberger and the Steelers were finished when backup quarterback Landry Jones threw an interception with less than two minutes left in the game and the Bengals leading by a point.

But then Bengals running back Jeremy Hill inexplicably tried fighting for extra yardage without two arms guarding the football as if it were precious cargo and linebacker Ryan Shazier forced a fumble that the Steelers recovered deep in their own territory.

"Ben and I have been together for nine years," Steelers coach Mike Tomlin said after the game. "We kind of looked at each other and said now or never."

Roethlisberger re-entered the game with a bad shoulder that prevented him from making deep throws. Fortunately for the Steelers, Burfict decided it was time to stake his claim to player of the game for each team.

LOVE STILL CONQUERS ALL

Bee Huss made an appearance in the first chapter of the book with her toast at the Steelers' tailgate I visited. She is, to recap, an avowed Browns hater who happens to be married to a Bengals fan. I wondered if the Steelers 18–16 win over the Bengals in the 2016 AFC playoffs had caused any friction between Bee and her husband, Matt, and I am happy to report it did not.

Bee, who lives outside of Toledo, Ohio, did not attend the game because of a cold as well as her concern that it might get a little ugly for Steelers fans at Paul Brown Stadium if Pittsburgh beat Cincinnati.

Matt Huss went to the game and he and Bee talked about it afterward but they have too much of a foundation after almost 30 years of marriage to let it come between them.

"We're used to it," Bee said of a mixed marriage when it comes to the AFC North. "It's never mean or nasty or anything like that. He says, 'When is it going to be our time? I'd be happy with winning one Super Bowl.'"

Burfict had knocked Roethlisberger out of the game with his third-quarter sack and then made the interception that appeared to deliver Bengals coach Marvin Lewis' first postseason win.

But with the Steelers on the Bengals' 47-yard line and just 22 seconds left to play, the game turned on an incomplete pass. Roethlisberger's pass sailed past Antonio Brown but Burfict leveled the Steelers' wideout in the head with a running shoulder hit.

That drew a 15-yard penalty for unnecessary roughness, and the Bengals gave the Steelers another gift when cornerback Adam Jones was flagged for unsportsmanlike conduct for bumping a referee.

Tomlin wasted little time sending out Boswell, the Steelers' unsung hero in 2015, for the game-winning field goal. His kick split the uprights, leaving the Bengals an entire off-season to chew on their most dispiriting loss to the despised Steelers in franchise history.

Days after the improbable turn of events in Cincinnati it was still hard to make sense of the ending. Jones made the absurd claim that Brown had been faking his injury after the Burfict hit. He issued a public apology to Brown after the latter could not play the following week against the Broncos because of a concussion, and Burfict was later suspended by the NFL for the first three regular-season games of 2016.

If I am Roger Goodell I have video copies of the Burfict hit on standby for anyone who gripes about the NFL commissioner trying to turn the game into flag football with his player safety initiatives.

That play is Exhibit A for why Goodell needs to protect the players from themselves.

Burfict was clearly trying to take Brown out of the game—and he tried to find some loophole that allows for a shoulder instead of a helmet to blow up a defenseless player.

The 2015 season might have changed the dynamics of the Steelers' AFC North rivalries. The Browns are the definition of a hot mess and have not been consistently competitive against the Steelers since the NFL returned to Cleveland in 1999.

The Bengals, meanwhile, have been ready to win for years now but have yet to prove they can go through the Steelers or other perennial contenders in the AFC.

Has Steelers-Bengals surpassed Steelers-Browns as Pittsburgh's second-most contentious rivalry? Stay tuned.

. . . .

A Steelers Haven in Cincinnati

Steelers fans traveling to Cincinnati for a game can find friendly confines near the University of Cincinnati. Martino's on the Vine touts itself as "Cincinnati's Home of the Pittsburgh Steelers," and it's hard to dispute that claim.

Marty Angiulli, affectionately known as "Mop," started the bar/restaurant in the early 1990s after he and his wife followed their son, Marty Jr., to the University of Cincinnati, where he played football.

They established a popular spot just off campus and got to know a young assistant coach by the name of Mike Tomlin. Cincinnati was Tomlin's last college stop before he got his NFL break with the Tampa Bay Buccaneers in 2001, and he stops in Martino's if his schedule permits when the Steelers visit the Bengals.

The walls at Martino's are covered with Steelers paraphernalia, and kielbasa, homemade pizza pierogis, and salad with French fries are all on the menu. Iron City and I.C. Light are served at Martino's as is Rolling Rock, which is native to Latrobe, and Yuengling, which is from the eastern part of Pennsylvania.

Martino's draws a couple of hundred fans for Steelers games and its 30 TVs come in handy for newcomers who find regulars at their normal spots along the bar or in booths that still provide a clear view of the game.

"Mop," who spends half the year in Cincinnati and half in the Pittsburgh suburb of Vandergrift, has one rule for Steelers games: no Bengals fans allowed.

"We used to let them in and we were always breaking up fights," Angiulli said. "I'm getting too old to break up fights."

Rivalries Outside the AFC North

Yesteryear

The precursor to the contentiousness and competitiveness of Steelers-Ravens unfolded in the 1970s—and specifically when the Steelers made their move.

Pittsburgh and Oakland played 11 times from 1970 to '77, with the Raiders winning six of those games. Five of those meetings took place in the postseason, three from 1974–76. All three times the team that emerged from those games also won the Super Bowl.

The rivalry, meanwhile, became so nasty that it ended up in a courtroom.

Frenchy Fuqua poses with the towel that articulates his stance on the mystery of the "Immaculate Reception."
(Photo courtesy of Frenchy Fuqua)

Raiders safety George Atkinson sued Chuck Noll for defamation after the Steelers coach said the NFL needed to get rid of the "criminal element" following a 1976 game in which an Atkinson hit away from the play left wide receiver Lynn Swann with a concussion.

Atkinson lost the case but nothing better epitomized the raw feelings between the AFC powers, and all of that could be traced to December 23, 1972.

That is the day the Steelers won the first playoff game in franchise history—on the play that has turned into the sports equivalent of the Zapruder film. What is known as the "Immaculate Reception" to Steelers fans is still called the "Immaculate Deception" by former Raiders linebacker Phil Villapiano.

At the crux of the dispute is whether Steelers running back Frenchy Fuqua or Raiders safety Jack Tatum touched the ball first, right before it ricocheted back to Franco Harris. Harris' shoestring grab and subsequent 60-yard touchdown reception delivered a 13–7 win, and feelings after that game were so hard that it strained at least one friendship.

Fuqua and Raiders tight end Raymond Chester, former teammates at Morgan State, had been close friends prior to the most famous play in NFL history. They stopped talking that day and the incommunicado lasted for years.

A significant thaw between players on each side occurred around 2004, Fuqua said, at an NFL golf outing in Nashville, Tennessee.

There were 12 players, he said, from that game at the outing, including Tatum and Chester. Both sides started arguing almost immediately about the play and the conversations led to a detour.

"We all ended up at a bar and none of us showed up to the golf outing the next day," Fuqua said with a laugh. "I have not been invited to that tournament since but we really talked."

His conversations with Tatum, who passed away in 2010, continued and they even appeared at some banquets together. The two, Fuqua said, made peace with one another as well as the play.

"We both exchanged versions to each other," Fuqua said. "He said he didn't know what happened. All he knew is that he was trying to tear my head off. I said, 'Well, we're going to keep it that no one knows. I'll never tell.'"

Fuqua and Chester, meanwhile, stay in touch and occasionally talk on the phone. Of course, they still argue about the legality of Harris' touchdown, but more in fun now.

"I think that hate—since all of us have become senior citizens—has faded a little bit," Fuqua said, "and it's just a story now."

* * *

A rivalry that once ranked up there with any of them for the Steelers had the air taken out of it by forces beyond their control.

In 2002, the NFL broke up the six-team AFC Central, taking the Tennessee Titans and Jacksonville Jaguars out of the division and moving them to the newly created AFC South.

Black and Gold fans coming of age now look at the Titans as just another team, but the Steelers have a long history with that organization.

The Titans had been the Houston Oilers before moving to Nashville in 1997, and the Steelers beat the Oilers in back-to-back AFC Championship Games en route to the final two Super Bowls of the 1970s.

Chuck Noll's last playoff win came against the Oilers and it cemented 1989 as one of his best coaching jobs while costing Jerry Glanville his job. The Steelers started that season 0–2 and lost to the Browns and Bengals by a combined score of 92–10.

Noll stayed the course and the Steelers won nine of their last 14 games to qualify for the postseason. They weren't given much chance to win in Houston's "House of Pain," but the Steelers took the Oilers into overtime.

Rod Woodson forced a fumble that gave the Steelers excellent field position but they couldn't move the ball and Noll opted to punt rather than try a long field call. Defensive coordinator Rod Rust, however, told Noll that he didn't think his gassed defense could hold off the Oilers if they got the ball again. Noll took a timeout and then sent Gary Anderson to attempt a 51-yard field goal.

Anderson made it, giving the Steelers a 26–23 win and Noll no small measure of satisfaction. A couple of years earlier he had scolded Glanville during a post-game handshake for what he considered dirty play by the Oilers.

That started a feud between the coaches that carried over to the players. After the Steelers upset the Oilers in the wild-card round of the playoffs, offensive tackle Tunch Ilkin, who never talked trash, could not resist letting his opponents hear about it.

"How's the pain, baby?" a pumped Ilkin shouted after Anderson's field goal quieted the Astrodome crowd. "How bad does it hurt now?"

Alas for the Steelers, the Oilers handed them a painful loss after the organization had relocated and become the Titans.

The Titans won a crazy game that had a little bit of everything, including a controversial finish. The Steelers fell behind 14–0 but then scored 20 unanswered points. The back-and-forth game went into overtime, where Joe Nedney kicked field goals three different times before one counted and gave the Titans a 34–31 win.

Nedney's 31-yard field goal attempt split the uprights but it didn't count because the Steelers called timeout before the snap. He missed his next kick but it didn't count after Dewayne Washington was flagged for running into Nedney.

Nedney drilled the 26-yard mulligan he received, giving the Oilers/Titans their only playoff win over the Steelers.

Present

Go to a sports bar that has a lot of Steelers fans in it when the Patriots are playing and it takes mere minutes to experience the general dislike to visceral hatred of New England. This really struck me a week after the Steelers' heartbreaking loss at Denver in the 2015 AFC playoffs. The Patriots were playing the Broncos and the crowd at a Pittsburgh-area Primanti Brothers where I watched the AFC Championship Game went nuts any time the team that had eliminated the Steelers did something good. Even more telling: All it took was an extended shot of Patriots quarterback Tom Brady on the TV screens for calls of "Whiner!" or "Cheater!" to echo throughout the bar.

The Patriots are easily the Steelers' most despised rival outside of the AFC North, and a lot of that is rooted in New England owning Pittsburgh since Brady and coach Bill Belichick started winning Super Bowls together in the 2000s.

The Patriots are 8–3 against the Steelers since Brady's emergence, including 2–0 in the AFC Championship Game.

The Patriots drilled the Steelers in 2007 after safety Anthony Smith's infamous guarantee that Pittsburgh would hand New England its first loss of the season. Brady again strafed the Steelers in 2013, throwing for 432 yards and four touchdowns in the Patriots' 55–31 romp in Foxboro.

The Steelers have beaten Brady just twice in 10 games against him from 2001 to 2015, and Black and Gold fans are as put off by how the Patriots have won as much as they are by how frequently they have won. I suppose this makes them like a lot of fans in NFL cities across the country.

The Patriots' four Super Bowl titles since 2000 have come under a cloud of suspicion since New England has continually shown it will do anything to gain an edge. The team has been punished by the NFL for illegally taping opponents and deflating footballs in the 2014 AFC Championship Game.

Some Steelers players have publicly questioned whether the Patriots knew what offensive plays they were running in the 2004 AFC Championship Game. And as recently as 2015 the Steelers said there were headset communications issues in a 28–21 loss at Gillette Stadium.

My take? Belichick is on a very short list of the greatest football coaches of all time and Brady might be the greatest quarterback of all time. The best analogy I heard after the Deflategate controversy is that Belichick is the smartest kid in class who still feels the need to write the answers to a test on his arm.

The perception of the Patriots as cheaters is fair, but show me a team that doesn't try to gain an advantage. New England has simply stretched those bounds more than any team since becoming the first organization to win four Super Bowls with the same head coach and quarterback since the Steelers with Chuck Noll and Terry Bradshaw.

The good news for the Steelers: the window is starting to close on Brady's career. The bad news for the Steelers: they are running out of time to saddle Belichick and Brady with the losses that would make the rivalry less one-sided in this century.

Road Trippin'

Black and Gold fans need to make at least one road trip if only to see the kind of support the Steelers receive when they travel to a game. A crush of fans congregates at the team hotel to see the Steelers arrive and then see the team buses off the next day.

And Terrible Towels have long taken over stadiums of teams whose own fans are willing to sell tickets. Here are 10 trips to make outside of the AFC North:

Green Bay: Lambeau Field has an unmistakable aura and should be on any sports fan's bucket list of places to see. The Steelers don't play here often—they have visited Green Bay just twice since 2005—but my trip to Lambeau Field in 2013 has stuck with me and one scene in particular. I drove past a bar on the way into the stadium and despite temperatures that were close to freezing the patio was packed with fans who drank beer outside as if it were July—and didn't seem to have a care in the world. The Packers' history, the small-town setting of Green Bay and the enthusiasm of Cheesehead-wearing fans make Lambeau a must-stop.

New Orleans: As a good friend of mine once put it, you can do anything on Bourbon Street within reason. I experienced Bourbon Street for the first time in 2010 when the Steelers played a Sunday night game in New Orleans on Halloween. Bourbon Street was absolutely nuts the night before the game and I'll never forget seeing Steelers defensive end Nick Eason there. Eason walked among the revelers who were dressed in all manner of costumes, simply taking in the spectacle, and for good reason. Bourbon Street is worth seeing even if, like Eason, you are on a business trip.

San Francisco: The NFL will have a presence in northern California no matter what happens with the Raiders in the future, and San Francisco alone is worth seeing. There are so many attractions in this spectacular city with its signature trolleys, none better than Alcatraz. Ferries run regularly to the island that once housed America's most notorious prison and is all the more forbidding when it is shrouded in fog. The history of Alcatraz, which closed as a federal penitentiary in 1963, is fascinating. If you go at night it is downright eerie.

Dallas: AT&T Stadium, Jerry Jones' personal playground, is a monument to splendor and excess—the high-definition video scoreboard alone is 175 feet wide—which makes it totally Dallas. Dealey Plaza, the epicenter of John F. Kennedy's assassination in 1963, still abounds with morbid intrigue. Comprehensive tours are conducted at the Texas Book Depository where Lee Harvey Oswald fired the shots that killed Kennedy. Outside, on the infamous grassy knoll, there are conspiracy theorists who will tell you not to believe what you hear on the tours—and are more than happy to offer you their versions.

Seattle: I have to qualify this by saying Seattle is the only NFL city I never visited in the course of covering the Steelers and that it is not the easiest place to get to if you are flying. But the scenery is supposedly spectacular and no NFL venue is louder than CenturyLink Stadium. Yeah, it rains a lot there, but gray, chilly days are a Pittsburgh signature, so weather shouldn't deter Steelers fans from visiting Seattle.

Chicago: Soldier Field is the oldest NFL stadium and, like Lambeau Field, it conjures up memories of so many great players. George Halas. Dick Butkus. Gale Sayers. Walter Payton. All are part of the great history at Soldier Field. Imagine tailgating with bratwurst and beer and then watching two of the NFL's flagship franchises play at one of its most venerable stadiums. And Chicago, even with its harsh winters, is as good as it gets as far as visiting or living in a big city. An added bonus, if the schedules align, is catching a Cubs game at Wrigley Field.

Kansas City: Another heartland destination that is dripping with NFL history and boasts fans that are as passionate as they come.

Arrowhead Stadium turns into a sea of red on game days and the place is as loud as any NFL venue this side of Seattle. The game-day experience alone makes this a worthwhile trip and if you can't find a good steak or ribs joint while visiting Kansas City, that's on you.

San Diego: This city has to be a meteorologist's dream. Simply forecast clear skies and temperatures in the 70s and 80s and there is a good chance it will happen. No city in America consistently has better weather than San Diego, and tourist attractions include the San Diego Zoo and the city's Gaslight district, which is packed with restaurants and bars. The Chargers' future in San Diego remains tenuous but it would be a shame if the franchise relocated.

Jacksonville: Any of the three NFL cities in Florida is worth visiting if the Steelers are playing in the Sunshine State in November or December. Miami has South Beach, Tampa has Ybor City, and each is worth experiencing for the nightlife and people watching. Don't underestimate Jacksonville Beach, which has plenty of hotspots within a contained area right on the Atlantic Ocean. Golfers willing to shell out some money have the opportunity to play TPC Sawgrass in Ponte Vedra Beach. The course is home to the Players Championship and perhaps the most famous par–3 in the world. No. 17 plays not more than 100 yards, give or take a first down, but the island green can be difficult to hit. Dunk a few in the water and that merely puts you in the same company as those who play golf for a living.

New York: New York sports fans are a species all their own—and I mean this as a compliment—and experiencing New York City makes this trip worth making whether the Steelers are playing the Jets or Giants at MetLife Stadium. There is an undeniable energy about New York and there is no shortage of tourist attractions. Ground Zero gives visitors a chance to pay homage to the men and women who defined bravery on 9/11 in the terrorist attacks that toppled the World Trade Center.

The Steelers in Hollywood

The Steelers have long cultivated an image of a hard-hitting, physical team that reflects the sensibilities of their blue-collar city. But the Steelers have some history with the silver screen and no one has had more of a presence on it than former quarterback Terry Bradshaw.

Bradshaw started appearing in movies while he was still playing and has had small roles in a handful of movies, including *The Cannonball Run*. Bradshaw's biggest role on screen came in 2006 when he played Matthew McConaughey's father in *Failure to Launch*.

Bill Cowher has appeared in a handful of movies, including *The Waterboy*, an Adam Sandler flick that is so bad it's funny.

Even longtime Steelers beat writer Ed Bouchette has gotten into the act. Bouchette, who has covered the Steelers since the 1980s for the *Pittsburgh Post-Gazette*, has a cameo in *Invincible* to his credit.

"Mean Joe" Crushes It with Coca-Cola

The Steelers owned the 1970s, but it wasn't until the end of the decade that Joe Greene became a national figure.

And "Mean Joe" went Hollywood to spread what players, agents, and those in the marketing game today refer to as their "brand."

Well, sort of.

Mount Vernon, New York, and a small municipal stadium were the actual sites where one of the most feared defensive players of his era, a young boy, a grass-stained white Steelers jersey, and a bottle of Coke came together to produce one of the most famous TV commercials of all time.

In the commercial, a limping Greene stopped in a dimly lit tunnel when young Tommy Okon, acing his role of a timid boy approaching his hero, offered his bottle of Coke to "Mean Joe." Greene chugged the soft drink, tossed his jersey to the kid, and then flashed a smile.

The commercial, which first aired in 1979, remains the standard for advertising executives, though its simplicity belied what actually went into making it.

Greene said two full days were needed to shoot the commercial—it was supposed to take half a day—and that he drank 18 bottles of Coke because there were so many takes.

"Boy, that was terrible," Greene said in a video interview with Coca-Cola.

The end result turned out to be sweeter than anyone could have foreseen and the commercial humanized Greene. Fans who had been hesitant to approach Greene off the field were much more willing to ask for an autograph, he said, after the commercial morphed into an advertising phenomenon.

Greene said Coca-Cola considered Roger Staubach, Ed "Too Tall" Jones, Tony Dorsett, and Jack Lambert for the commercial. And it came down to the two Steelers defensive stars for the role that went to Greene.

"Lambert didn't have any teeth," Greene said with a grin. "He wouldn't have looked good on TV."

Like Father, Like Son

Tom Okon caught a jersey from "Mean" Joe Greene. Three decades later, one of his sons caught passes from another Steelers legend.

The Steelers brought Okon and Greene together in 2009 for a 30th anniversary celebration of their famed Coca-Cola commercial, recognizing them for winning the Clio Award, one of advertising's highest honors. Okon reunited with Greene before the game at Heinz Field and introduced him to his wife and four children. Okon and his young son, Scott, were playing catch on the field when the past connected with the present.

"Who kind of steps in front of the pass intentionally but Hines Ward," Okon recalled. "He goes to throw it to him and kind of lobs it to him underhand and I say, 'No, he can catch; you can let one go.' So he had a quick little [game of] catch with my son, not knowing who we are, just a father and son on the field."

The experience forged an unlikely bond between Greene and Okon, who was nine years old when he starred in the commercial that he is still asked about to this day.

The irony is that Okon, in a total coincidence when he was cast for the role, had significant ties to Pittsburgh. Both of his parents had grown up in Western Pennsylvania, and his father attended Pitt while his mother went to Carnegie Mellon University before they married and relocated to New York City to work in TV.

"Any kid who was a football fan in the '70s you knew the Steelers, you knew the Steel Curtain, and you knew the name Mean Joe Greene," Okon recalled. "It was a different world, no ESPN and all that, so I didn't know what he looked like. I just knew the name."

Greene left his intimidating aura in Pittsburgh for the commercial shoot and Okon said he couldn't have worked with a nicer person. Apparently Greene felt the same way. That Christmas he sent Okon an autographed Steelers jersey, and their story didn't end there.

A couple of years later Okon went to visit his brother, a graduate student at Carnegie Mellon, and took Greene up on his invitation to call if he was ever in Pittsburgh.

Greene invited the Okon brothers to Three Rivers Stadium and after greeting them said he would catch up with them after a "friend" showed them around. The younger Okon felt a twinge of disappointment, thinking an intern would give them a tour of the stadium.

Their guide turned out to be none other than Steelers owner Art Rooney.

"I'm a kid, I don't know owners at this point, I don't know what an iconic guy this is," Okon said. "So Art Rooney gives us a tour and I remember my brother grabbing me and going, 'You don't know what a big deal this is but you'll be talking about this for the rest of your life.' Sure enough I'm talking about it for the rest of my life."

Okon grew out of acting shortly after he started attending high school. Today he owns Castle Rock Marble and Granite, which is about half a mile from where he shot the Coca-Cola commercial.

Okon and Greene stay in touch and they reunited in January 2016, when they took part in a special for the 50th anniversary of the Super Bowl.

The funny thing looking back, Okon said, is he might have never starred in the commercial had Coca-Cola cast a Cowboys player in Greene's role. Okon and his parents, after all, rooted for the Steelers but they were diehard New York Giants fans.

"We joked if it was Staubach [in the commercial] I don't know if they would have let me do it," Okon said. "That's how much we hated the Cowboys."

Steelers and the Dark Knight

Thomas Tull, a self-made businessman, hit it big when he ventured into entertainment and became a major player in Hollywood. Tull is the CEO and chairman of Legendary Pictures, which has produced and financed the *Dark Knight* and *Hangover* series, as well as *We Are Marshall*.

Tull grew up in upstate New York but is a lifelong Steelers fan. He crossed off the ultimate item on a fan's bucket list when he became an owner of his favorite team in 2008. Tull bought a piece of the Steelers when the NFL enforced a rule that prohibits league owners from also having gaming interests.

Tull and other investors helped Dan and Art Rooney II maintain control of the Steelers by buying from the Rooney brothers who sold their shares of the organization. Tull has since been as visible as any minority owner in sports.

He attends games when his schedule permits and usually wears a No. 58 jersey in homage to Jack Lambert. Tull also brought two of his passions together in 2011 for *The Dark Knight Rises.*

A handful of players as well as Steelers director of football and business administration Omar Khan and former coach Bill Cowher were cast in a scene filmed at Heinz Field.

No one had a bigger role than Hines Ward, who returns the opening kickoff in a game as the field implodes behind him. Just as cool is the black-and-gold clad fans in the stands—the Gotham Rogues apparently share colors with the Steelers—and the UPMC sign that is clearly visible on the Heinz Field scoreboard.

Hines Ward's Other Championship Moves

I never thought covering the Steelers would lead me to a block of studios in Hollywood on May 24, 2011. But there I was—and I admit grudgingly—the night Hines Ward and Kym Johnson took the stage in the finals of *Dancing With the Stars*.

The showcase was perfect for Ward, who loves challenges, and cameras, and had the foresight to know that going on *Dancing With the Stars* near the end of his playing career would only raise his profile off the field.

Covering him on the final night was not so ideal for a football scribe on deadline for the *Pittsburgh Tribune-Review*. Reporters were stashed in a room with a TV for the final night and it didn't take long to realize I was completely out of place. An entertainment writer sitting next to me asked me for information on Ward and I started rattling off his Steelers history and statistics. She politely but firmly interrupted me after she had some basics to let me know she wasn't writing Ward's life story. Yeah, gotcha.

After Ward and Johnson won, they were whisked from one reporter to the next as if they were going through the reverse of a wedding receiving line. I didn't exactly rate as a high priority among the entertainment media there and found myself near the end of a long line with a promise that Ward and Johnson would get to me if time permitted.

It quickly dawned on me that I had no chance of getting time with the winning duo so I called an audible. I simply hovered, as unobtrusive as possible, behind reporters near the front of the line and scribbled down quotes with my deadline looming.

I later got Ward for a couple of minutes for a second-day story but covering *Dancing With the Stars* checked off no boxes on my bucket list. And the trip only reminded me how terrifying it is to drive on the Los Angles freeway in a compact rental car.

The Steelers-Giants Link

Rooney Mara was nominated for an Academy Award in 2011 and her exquisite portrayal of the troubled protagonist in *The Girl with the Dragon Tattoo* also brought attention to her unique connection to the NFL.

She is the great-granddaughter of Steelers founder Art Rooney and Giants founder Tim Mara. Her father, Chris, is the Giants' senior vice president of player personnel, and her mother, Kathleen, is Tim Rooney's daughter.

Tim Rooney is one of Art Rooney's five sons, making Rooney Mara the niece of Steelers chairman Dan Rooney and a first cousin of Steelers president Art Rooney II.

If her name evokes NFL royalty that is because Tim and Wellington Mara and Art and Dan Rooney are the only father-son duos in the Pro Football Hall of Fame—and because compromises between the Rooneys and Maras helped shape the NFL.

The Rooneys convinced the Maras in the early 1960s to split national TV revenue evenly among all clubs so smaller-market teams could compete financially. Almost a decade later the Maras prodded the Rooneys into a move of the Steelers from the National Conference to the newly formed American Conference even though Dan Rooney opposed the move following the NFL-AFL merger.

The relationship between the Maras and Rooneys remains strong though there is one place their respective franchises aren't close. The Giants hold a 46–30–3 advantage over the Steelers in their all-time series. The Giants' 46 victories are the third-most by a Steelers opponent after the Browns (58) and the Eagles (47).

Turning Art Rooney's Story into a Movie

he Chief, the play that expertly captures the life story of Steelers founder Art Rooney, hasn't gone Hollywood quite yet, but Tom Chaffee is working on it.

Chaffee is a managing partner of The Chief Partners and the group has at least ensured Rooney's story will exist in perpetuity with the play having run its course after almost a decade. *The Chief* is now a movie—it is available on DVD for $19.99—and it is a must-add to a Steelers fan's video library, along with broadcasts of the six Super Bowl victories and various other games.

The remake of *The Chief* preserves the integrity of the play—Pittsburgh native Tom Atkins, no stranger to Hollywood, performed sublimely as Rooney—while also enhancing it.

"The movie's better than the play simply because we were able to capture what we felt were the best performances of Tom," said Chaffee, the executive producer of the movie.

Chaffee and his production team did that, after securing movie rights in 2009, by filming *The Chief* at Shadyside Academy with a crew of 30–35 people and an audience. The setting and the live audience kept the feel of a play. The freedom to shoot scenes as many times as they wanted ensured they would get Atkins at his best throughout *The Chief*.

They also added interviews at the end of the movie with Dan and Art Rooney Jr. and former Steelers players among others to complement the one-man play.

WPXI-TV in Pittsburgh aired the movie in August 2015. Chaffee is hoping for a national airing of *The Chief,* something the NFL can tie into a celebration such as the start of a new season or the Super Bowl.

"There's so many people that need to see this film that haven't," Chaffee said.

No argument here.

The Steelers and the Media

Pittsburgh is one of a dwindling number of cities with two newspapers and the *Post-Gazette* and *Tribune-Review* each has three writers who cover the Steelers on a daily basis as well as columnists and photographers who also travel with the team.

Former Steelers players Charlie Batch and Chris Hoke are part of the KDKA-TV team that covers the Steelers and televises their preseason games and Jerome Bettis hosts a weekly show on WPXI-TV.

Radio is still huge in Pittsburgh when it comes to the Steelers, whether it is pre-game shows or during the week, and a handful of players have their own shows on various outlets.

Coach Mike Tomlin makes it very clear to his players to watch what they say and that is code for "do not talk team business." Tomlin, like any NFL head coach, broadly defines what should be kept within the organization and that adds to the appeal of *The Ben Roethlisberger Show.*

Roethlisberger appears every week on 93.7 The Fan, an all-sports station in Pittsburgh, during the season and the veteran quarterback is almost always forthcoming, providing thoughtful and insightful answers.

Roethlisberger is generally everything Tomlin isn't in a media setting and part of me wonders if part of this isn't Big Ben tweaking his head coach a bit. Tomlin surely has to get exasperated with some of the things Roethlisberger says, particularly when he talks about an injury, but what is he going to do, bench him?

Like The Fan, the Steelers' Pittsburgh radio affiliates, 970-AM and WDVE-FM, provide a ton of team coverage. Tunch Ilkin and Craig Wolfley, former teammates who are part of the Steelers' radio broadcast team, host a weekday show on 970-AM from 10:00 AM to noon during the season and it stands out for several reasons.

Tunch and Wolf know each other as well as they do themselves, and they playfully bust on one another while also providing terrific analysis and insight on the Steelers. That comes from their background in the organization and the amount of work they put in watching film and practice and talking to players.

Civility, which is not always congruous with sports talk radio, is a staple of their show too. Tunch and Wolf are patient when a caller asks, well, not the brightest of questions and they are polite to callers instead of shouting them down or hanging up on them.

"We think it's important to be gracious to our callers even if they say things we don't believe in and we want to have a show that reflects who we are," Ilkin said. "We want to make sure we have a show where everyone can listen. If someone is in their car with their kid, they're not afraid something is going to be said. We want to have a show that honors God. We want people to feel like they can come to one of our Bible studies or one of our outings or one of our huddles. We invite people to come and lock arms with us and that's why the way we do our show, we're very intentional about it."

A Steelers Hub in...Florida

A man who does not like crowds is surrounded by them in a sense almost every hour of the day. That irony is not lost on Steelers Depot founder Dave Bryan.

"It is funny," Bryan said. "Social media gives you a chance to interact without personally interacting. It's almost like a fantasy world."

Dream world is more like it.

Bryan has parlayed his love of the Steelers, technological savvy and manic personality into a website that has taken off since he launched it in 2007.

Steelers Depot, which provides non-stop updates, analysis and in-depth breakdowns, has become so popular that Bryan hired a full-time writer in 2015 and also has several part-time scribes on his payroll.

Bryan declined to go into specifics on how his site became profitable enough to turn into a second career for him. The Pensacola, Florida, resident did say that Steelers Depot receives more than 2 million hits per month, a staggering number for a grass-roots website.

"It really has snowballed over the last three or four years," Bryan said.

A lot of that is because of Bryan himself.

He taught himself how to design and launch websites after retiring at the age of 40 following a successful real estate career. And Bryan has been in front of the curve when it comes to always-evolving social media.

He started blogging tirelessly before it became popular and has built a vast following in part because he never seems to stop.

Bryan is a recovering alcoholic and drug addict and he said a number of disorders flared up after he got clean. One of those is bipolar disorder, which Bryan said does not allow him to sleep more than five hours on the one day of the week he gets a significant amount of winks.

As a result, Bryan said, he spends 18–20 hours a day watching Pittsburgh sports and writing about the Steelers on his website and other social media outlets such as Twitter. The work is perfect for Bryan because he has an aversion to crowds and has only been to two Steelers games in his life.

TWO OF A KIND

Tunch Ilkin and Craig Wolfley are so inseparable that they still share everything from a cramped dorm room at training camp to a Twitter account. That doesn't mean they don't occasionally need a break from one another, as they found out during the most trying stretch of their Steelers playing careers. The team went 5–11 in 1988 and lost 10 of 11 games at one point. Tension that season boiled over between the best friends as they were walking to their gate in Pittsburgh International Airport for an away game.

Wolf told Tunch he looked like a preppie and the latter took offense. "What are you talking about?" Tunch fired back. "You look like yesterday's newspaper." The two started arguing and nearly came to blows in the airport. They went their separate ways but within 15 minutes found one another and started laughing. Even funnier is what they heard a woman say to her husband during their spat. "Look at them," she said. "No wonder they're losing. They're fighting amongst themselves."

He has tapped into something though, as Steelers Depot has more Twitter followers (49,100 as of May 2016) than every Steelers beat writer after the *Pittsburgh Post-Gazette's* Ed Bouchette, who is in the Pro Football Hall of Fame.

Steelers Depot's rise is as unique as Bryan's fierce allegiance to the Steelers and Pittsburgh sports in general.

Bryan was born in Pensacola and the only time he visited Pittsburgh he and his wife went to a Pirates baseball game. But his love of the Steelers started when he was just a youngster and Bryan wanted to tweak his dad, who rooted for the Cowboys,

Steelers Depot, a popular website for team news and analysis, caters to fans such as Bud Yoder of Lancaster, Pennsylvania.

Before long, he was a "full-fledged Yinzer" and that eventually led to a full-time gig doing something Bryan loves.

It helps that his writers are as passionate about the Steelers as Bryan is—the group makes 16 to 20 posts a day and does not recognize that there is an off-season—not to mention an understanding wife.

"Is she a sports fan? Absolutely not," said Bryan. "She could tell you the key players on the [Steelers] but she doesn't keep up with the record or sit with me and watch games. She knows it's just part of who I am."

Chapter 6

Appreciating What Isn't Always So Apparent

Steelers chairman Dan Rooney can stack his legacy against any sports owner.

He has been instrumental in the Steelers winning an NFL-best six Super Bowls and the organization becoming a national brand. He helped shape the NFL into a powerful, billion-dollar enterprise but is just as proud of the "Rooney Rule," which mandates interview opportunities for minorities when it comes to head-coaching and executive openings.

Oh, and yeah, Rooney also served as the United States' Ambassador to Ireland from 2009 to 2013, fulfilling a dream of serving both his country and his ancestral homeland. A book could be written about Rooney and his accomplishments— and would have been had "DMR," as he is sometimes referred to at Steelers headquarters, not done it himself. *Dan Rooney: My 75 Years with the Pittsburgh Steelers and the NFL* came out in 2008 and is cited multiple times in this book.

The thrust of this chapter isn't to laud transcendent figures like Rooney as much as it is to recognize others who deserve credit for critical contributions as well as

---

EXTRA POINTS

Gay Makes Mark on the Field Too

His teammates gave him the nickname "Big Play Willie Gay" early in his career. It just took some time for Steelers cornerback William Gay to grow into the moniker.

Gay, a fifth-round draft pick in 2007, intercepted three passes in his first five seasons with the Steelers before signing with the Arizona Cardinals as an unrestricted free agent in 2012. The Cardinals released Gay after one season and he returned to the Steelers.

The signing that lurked under the radar turned out to be one of the better ones that the Steelers have made in free agency. Gay returned five consecutive interceptions for touchdowns from 2013 to '15, setting an NFL record. He also emerged as the Steelers' top cornerback in his second stint with the team and showed something to fans who had relentlessly criticized Gay earlier in his career.

---

the organization's impact beyond football. It also takes a look at some of the harsh truths of the game, from the enormous physical cost it can exact to the reality that most players don't get to go out on their own terms.

Giving Back off the Field

Bill Priatko played just one season for the Steelers but that didn't stop the team from inviting him to represent the 1950s when they held an 80th-anniversary celebration in 2012.

He is the only one in a photo taken by the Steelers whose numbers are gold instead of white, and Priatko goes back far enough that he played for the Steelers in 1957 and was roommates during Cleveland Browns training camp two years later with a rookie defensive back named Dick LeBeau.

Priatko and LeBeau remain close friends to this day, and he has also maintained a correspondence and friendship with Bart Starr throughout the years from his short stint with the Green Bay Packers.

There probably isn't a friendlier or more well-meaning person than Priatko. He is the type of person who knows everybody and doesn't have a bad word to say about anybody.

It is little wonder than that he developed a friendship with Steelers founder Art Rooney and one with the Rooney family that endures.

What tugs at Priatko's emotions is when he talks about the Rooneys' connection with his son, Dan.

Dan Priatko played football for Army and graduated from West Point in 1984. He completed training as an Army Ranger and that is what ultimately saved his life.

Dan Priatko and his sister, Debbie, were driving home from West Point after a visit when they hit an ice storm near Hazelton, Pennsylvania. Dan lost control of the car and the driver's side rammed right into a cement abutment.

Dan wasn't expected to make it—his sister escaped with minor injuries—and then spent seven months in a coma. He survived the crash because he was in such great physical condition but it left him paralyzed on one side of his body and he is largely confined to a wheelchair.

The Rooneys stayed in touch with him through the years and Art Rooney Jr. still writes to Dan at least once a week. He didn't forget to send a letter either when he and his wife were vacationing once in Russia. Dan Rooney has also supported the family and he wrote a letter of recommendation that helped get David Priatko, Dan's younger brother, into West Point.

"It means so much to Dan," Bill Priatko said. "He has so much respect for the Rooney family because of the way they are with him. The Rooneys are special. They really are."

That goes back to Art Rooney.

The Steelers founder always instilled in his players the importance of not just working in Pittsburgh but also getting involved outside of football. That helps explain why so many players, particularly from the 1970s, became invested in the community and stayed in Pittsburgh after they retired.

"He would ask us to join various charitable efforts that the Steelers were taking on, like the Salvation Army," former Steelers linebacker Andy Russell said of Art Rooney, "and it was making a statement to us that it it's good to give back to the community, that you can't just take the money and run."

Nobody embraced that sentiment more than cornerback Mel Blount.

The Pro Football Hall of Famer has maintained a strong presence in the Pittsburgh area—the guy wearing the cowboy hat who still looks like he could lock down NFL wide receivers, that's Blount—and he runs a group home in Western Pennsylvania for young men.

Blount's eponymous organization offers shelter, structure, and hope to abused or neglected boys. And its success has added to the legacy of Blount, who was such a physically dominant player that the NFL changed the rules regarding contact between defensive backs and receivers in the late 1970s.

The Mel Blount Youth Home is a non-profit organization and one of its main fundraisers also qualifies as a Steelers bucket list item. Blount serves up himself annually for a roast that is a black-tie affair and a ton of laughs.

A former Steelers teammate always serves as a master of ceremonies for the Mel Blount Roast and there is nothing like listening to stories from the 1970s while helping a great cause. It is a measure of respect that Blount commands for his off-the-field work that former quarterback Terry Bradshaw, who has had a complicated relationship with the city of Pittsburgh, returned in 2016 to lead the roast as master of ceremonies.

Charlie Batch is among this era of Steelers players who have given back to the community and, like Blount, he does more than just raise money and awareness for charitable causes. Batch grew up in Homestead, about a 10-minute drive from the Steelers' practice facility, and he signed with his hometown team in 2002 after four seasons in Detroit. Batch gave the Steelers one of the most reliable backup quarterbacks in the NFL and also grew his foundation.

The Best of the Batch Foundation now promotes education in a six-county area, and Batch tries to reel in kids like he did defenders during a 15-year NFL career with a good play-action fake.

"We're an educational foundation and we focus on reading/computer literacy," said Batch, who played for the Steelers from 2002 to 2012 and won some critical games for them. "What we do is trick their mind and use sports in some cases to draw the kids in. It's a lot easier to say, 'Hey, come play basketball.' We'll get 360 kids to come play basketball and then it's 'Oh, by the way, you need to read a book and attend four mandatory study halls.' It's a lot easier to do it that way than, 'Hey, meet me at the Carnegie Library, we're going to read a book.' I'd be lucky to get 20 kids."

The Batch Foundation also offers a lifeline for troubled kids who have been kicked out of school.

It operates an alternative school program at the foundation's Munhall facility and Batch and his colleagues work with teachers, principals, and even judges to help wayward kids get on track. Troubled kids can attend the school for up to six months while working with the foundation to get back into their regular schools and the response has been positive.

"We get calls from probation officers, judges saying, 'This kid needs help. Can you help map out a plan for him?'" Batch said. "The No. 1 goal is to build that trust immediately and say, 'Hey, look, we're here to help you,' and at that point we continue to move forward."

Part of that help is rewarding those who make it through the program.

In 2015, Batch's foundation awarded just over $100,000 in scholarship money to kids who had become academic success stories and gone to college.

Most of the Steelers' established players have started their own foundations and are involved in all manner of giving back, from quarterback Ben Roethlisberger buying canines for police and fire departments all over the country to cornerback William Gay lending a powerful voice and support to a cause that is deeply personal to him.

Gay lost his mother when he was a young boy after her boyfriend shot her and himself in the tragic culmination of an abusive relationship. He has since become one of sports' foremost advocates in combatting domestic violence, and Gay does more than just speak out in public service announcements.

He visits Pittsburgh shelters, sharing his story and providing hope while simply listening to battered women with the understanding of what they have endured.

Tunch Ilkin is another Steeler who goes above and beyond to help those who might feel like they have been forgotten by society.

Ilkin is the Steelers' color analyst for radio broadcasts and co-hosts a daily radio show with former teammate Craig Wolfley. He is also a devout Christian who ministers to those at the Light of Life Ministries, a homeless shelter on Pittsburgh's North Shore.

Ilkin, a sixth-round draft pick from Indiana State in 1980, developed into one of the Steelers' most indispensable offensive linemen in the 1980s and made a pair of Pro Bowls at the end of the decade.

His time with the Steelers, Ilkin said, shaped him even more as a person than a player because of veterans who defined glory as more than just what happened on a football field.

Their presence and a close friendship with Wolfley led Ilkin to convert to Christianity during his playing career. And in addition to his work at the Light of Life Ministries he is also the director of men's ministries at the South Hills Bible Chapel.

Ilkin never hesitates to share his journey as an example of what faith can do for a person.

"I was about as far from God as you can imagine," he said. "I was a druggie, a thief, a liar, and yet I met a bunch of guys on the Pittsburgh Steelers like Jon Kolb and Mike Webster and Donnie Shell and John Stallworth, guys who loved Jesus and loved each other. As I was processing all of this stuff that I was learning about God's love and his mercy and his grace and his plan, Wolf, who grew up in a Christian home, was right there helping me understand what I saw in these guys that was so attractive. I wanted to know about this God that loved me and these guys had a sense of purpose that was beyond football, Super Bowls, and Pro Bowls."

The sense of purpose that Ilkin developed led him to stay in Pittsburgh after his playing days were over. Like many retired players before him, Ilkin raised a family in the Pittsburgh area and now he can't imagine calling anywhere else home.

"I love the people, I love the neighborhoods, I love the non-profits that are making an impact here," Ilkin said. "You could name a hundred of them. What a privilege it is to be involved in what's happening here in Pittsburgh."

Rallying Behind One of Their Own

The figurative power of Jerome Bettis—his teammates badly wanted to get him a ring before he retired—helped drive the Steelers to the 2005 Super Bowl title.

They played for another teammate three seasons later on the way to a sixth Super Bowl title.

"It was about Aaron in '08," Brett Keisel said of fellow defensive end Aaron Smith. "His strength going through that whole situation, I think it soaked into all of us and all of us understood the role he played on our defense and how good he was."

Smith and his wife, Jaimie, lived a parent's nightmare that season after their son, Elijah, was diagnosed with a form of leukemia in late October, less than two months before his fifth birthday.

The way the Steelers rallied around Aaron Smith reflected the respect he commanded as a player and a person. And Keisel, whom Smith had mentored as a young player, went beyond playing for one of his best friends the season the Steelers won their most recent Super Bowl.

He has raised money for cancer research and cancer programs at Children's Hospital of Pittsburgh, making it a focal point of the charitable endeavors he has embraced throughout the years.

The gnarly beard that Keisel grew in 2010—and has become his signature—gets cut every February at Jergel's Rhythm Grille, just north of Pittsburgh. The charity event attracts Steelers fans and celebrity barbers, who take turns snipping Keisel's beard before he shaves most of it off.

The Sixth Annual Shear Da Beard—Keisel called it "Shear Da Yeard" because he grew out the beard for an entire year—raised more than $70,000 for Children's Hospital on February 11, 2016.

The event has raised more than $300,000 for Children's Hospital and less than a month before the 2016 edition Keisel received a powerful reminder of why it is so important.

He had returned from Denver following the Steelers' heartbreaking loss to the Broncos in an AFC playoff game and was getting his luggage at Pittsburgh International Airport when a young woman approached him. She told Keisel she was a cancer survivor who had been in remission for seven years and then thanked him.

"She said, 'I had leukemia as a child and I just want you to know that I really appreciate someone like you standing up for others that have had similar situations like I have,'" Keisel said. "It's awesome when those types of things happen to me and people come up and just say 'Thank you.' It's very touching and sometimes I don't really feel worthy because I feel like there's a lot more I could be doing. That's just how [the Steelers] do things here. We understand the importance of it, I think, and how much good it can do."

What really drives Keisel in raising money for cancer research and programs is the desire to give families what Aaron Smith and his family have experienced.

Elijah Smith has been in remission for years and Keisel said he is "doing great."

"He's playing sports and he's really sprouted up," Keisel said in January of 2016. "It's crazy to watch him grow and turn into this young man. It's just an incredible thing to see and know all of the things they've been through and seeing them come out on top."

Remembering Bill Nunn

A stately bench overlooking Chuck Noll Field at St. Vincent College has a small, rectangular plate on the back of it that reads, on three lines, "Bill Nunn, Jr. Steelers Super Scout 1924–2014."

Nunn, who passed away less than a week before the 2014 NFL Draft, sat in that location for years, watching the Steelers practice and chatting up legends like Joe Greene.

The memorial is fitting for several reasons. Like Nunn, it is understated. And, like Nunn's enormous contributions to the Steelers and the NFL, you have to look a little closer to appreciate it.

A sportswriter for the famed *Pittsburgh Courier* who knew and covered the likes of Jackie Robinson, Roberto Clemente, Joe Louis, and Muhammed Ali, Nunn joined the Steelers part time in 1967. He became a full-time scout shortly after the Steelers hired Chuck

Noll as their head coach in 1969 and the organization committed fully to building through the draft.

Nunn nurtured a pipeline to historically black colleges—he had picked All-American teams from those schools for the *Courier* for years, revealing his eye for talent—and is responsible for the best end-around in franchise history.

It came in 1974, when a group of scouts worked out Alabama A&M wide receiver John Stallworth in advance of the draft. Stallworth ran a pedestrian 40-yard dash on a wet field, underwhelming the scouts who were eager to get a close look at the small-school prospect.

All of scouts left the following day except for one. Nunn, feigning an illness, stayed back and took Stallworth to a track, where he turned in a considerably faster time in the 40-yard dash.

Nunn also asked the Alabama A&M coaches for Stallworth game films with the assurance that he would return them as soon as possible.

He mailed them back eventually but not before the Steelers went into the draft with better intelligence on Stallworth than any other team. That convinced Art Rooney Jr. that the Steelers could wait until after the first round to take Stallworth, even with Noll pushing for him over wide receiver Lynn Swann.

Rooney, who ran the scouting department, persuaded Noll to wait on Stallworth and the Steelers ended up with both him and Swann, getting the former in the fourth round.

Nunn also convinced the Steelers that year to sign an undrafted linebacker from South Carolina State named Donnie Shell. That draft and the free-agent signings of Shell and tight end Randy Grossman put the Steelers over the top, and they won four Super Bowls over the next six seasons.

"I have to make a confession," Rooney Jr. said of Shell. "I always said I scouted him too, [but] I went and looked at the old scouting reports years later and my name wasn't on the thing. That was a Bill Nunn creation."

The bench that overlooks Chuck Noll Field at St. Vincent College in Latrobe, Pennsylvania, is dedicated to the late, great Bill Nunn, one of the most significant figures in Steelers history.

Nunn remained a key voice in the Steelers' scouting and draft rooms until he passed away of complications from a stroke at the age of 89. His contributions to the NFL as a pioneer are chronicled in *The Color of Sundays*, written by *Pittsburgh Tribune-Review* investigative reporter Andrew Conte.

"I wouldn't be where I am today without someone like Bill Nunn blazing the trails in the scouting world for African Americans," Buffalo Bills general manager Doug Whaley said. "I'm in awe of the guy."

Whaley joined the Steelers as an intern after playing football at Pitt and working in the business world. He ascended through the scouting ranks with the Steelers and eventually rose to director of pro personnel.

He became the Bills' general manager in 2013 and landing the job only made Whaley appreciate even more what Nunn had done for him—before the two ever met and after that.

"He's sorely missed and I was blessed to have him as a mentor because he set the stage for me professionally and he helped me personally as a dad and a human being," Whaley said. "We loved when he came up to [training] camp and spent the night. It would be like Boy Scouts sitting around a campfire listening to a guy tell stories. It was ridiculous."

So is one of the Steelers memories that Whaley cherishes most.

When the Steelers made the Super Bowl in 2008, Whaley drove Nunn to Tampa, Florida, from Pittsburgh since the latter had stopped flying. Whaley could be forgiven as he listened to Nunn if he felt like one of the characters at the bus stop in *Forrest Gump*, sitting next to someone who had participated in so much history.

"Stories about how he would hang out with the Rat Pack in [Las] Vegas and football stories," Whaley said. "I can see it like it's yesterday."

Whaley would like to see one more chapter added to Nunn's remarkable story: induction into the Pro Football Hall of Fame.

"If you look at his impact, not only for the Steelers organization and being the head personnel scout for one of the great organizations with four Hall of Famers (in the same draft) and then winning six Super Bowls with the teams, he's got to be part of the conversation," Whaley said. "For him to open that pipeline to the historically black colleges when integration wasn't really a big part of college football and get those guys noticed, he was a conduit."

Another Steelers Trailblazer

John Mitchell has long been a big part of the Steelers' success.

The associate head coach/defensive line coach can be even more proud of the path he helped blaze on the way to Pittsburgh. Mitchell broke a significant color barrier at the University of Alabama in 1971 when he became the first African American to play in a football game for the Crimson Tide.

Mitchell had starred as a defensive lineman for an Arizona junior college after growing up in Mobile, Alabama, and could have taken a much easier route by signing with Southern Cal. Everything changed, however, when Trojans coach John McKay made a passing remark to Bear Bryant about a defensive player from Alabama that USC coveted, thinking there was no chance the Crimson Tide would recruit him.

Bryant, however, told his assistant coaches to go get Mitchell and he not only signed with Alabama, but flourished there. Mitchell earned All-American honors as a senior in Tuscaloosa and did not succumb to the pressure or isolation that came with breaking the color barrier at a flagship college football program in the Deep South.

Mitchell went into coaching in 1973, joining Bryant's staff, and he continued to break new ground. Mitchell became the first African American coordinator in the SEC in 1990 when LSU coach Mike Archer promoted him to defensive coordinator. Mitchell moved to the NFL in 1991 and spent three seasons in Cleveland before joining Bill Cowher's staff in 1994. He has been a fixture in Pittsburgh for more than two decades and is one of the top assistant coaches in the game.

Mitchell has consistently coached fronts that are among the toughest to run on in the NFL, and the Steelers did not allow a 100-yard rusher over a span of 34 games that bridged 2005 and 2007. Just as impressive is Mitchell's record of developing players. Aaron Smith, one of the best 3-4 defensive ends of his generation, arrived in Pittsburgh in 1999 as a fourth-round draft pick out of Division II Northern Colorado. Brett Keisel came to the Steelers as a seventh-round draft pick out of BYU in 2002. Keisel struggled so much during his first training camp that he considered leaving the team. He stayed, and like Smith developed into a cornerstone player on the defenses that led the Steelers to three Super Bowls and two world championships from 2005 to 2010.

"Mitch is very tough when you are a young player because he's taught so many great defensive linemen and he's figured out a way to teach guys that he knows works," Keisel said. "It's not pat you on the back and tell you it's okay. It's tough love and he tells you from the get-go that this isn't college, that this is a business for tough men, not only physically but mentally tough and you've got to find a way to be able to take his criticism and not dwell on it but use it for fuel, use it to get better because that's how you become good or great. When he knows that he can trust you and that you understand what we're trying to do collectively on Sunday he eases up."

Mitchell is much more than just a football coach and he prides himself on his interests outside of the game.

Mitchell is a wine connoisseur who also loves to read, particularly biographies on historical figures who overcame adversity. He can also claim that he once played pick-up basketball with the 42nd President of the United States, something that happened when Mitchell and Bill Clinton were at the University of Arkansas at the same time.

Dick Hoak's Excellent Adventure

Dick Hoak never made it to the Super Bowl as a player but he carved out a unique place in Steelers history.

He is the longest-tenured coach in Steelers history, and it is hard to imagine anyone topping his 35 seasons of service, during which he won five Super Bowl rings before leaving on his own terms.

Hoak played for the Steelers from 1961 to 1970 and twice led them in rushing. After retiring he took a job as a coach and physical education teacher at Wheeling Central Catholic in West Virginia, never expecting it to be a short stop.

But Hoak got a call from Pitt head coach Carl DePasqua one day after his first season at Wheeling Central Catholic asking him about joining the Panthers' staff. Hoak told DePasqua that he was interested and they agreed to set up a meeting.

A week later Hoak got another call while he was at school. This one was from Chuck Noll, who had coached Hoak for two seasons. Noll told him he would have an opening on his staff soon and Hoak again said he was interested.

He scheduled interviews with Pitt and the Steelers on the same day.

As fate would have it Hoak interviewed first with the Steelers, and after Noll agreed to give him a month to help Wheeling Catholic find a replacement, he accepted the job offer.

When he called DePasqua to cancel their interview, the former Steelers assistant coach told Hoak he would have been crazy not to accept Noll's offer. Less than two years later, Pitt fired DePasqua and his staff after the Panthers went 1–10, leaving Hoak to ponder the itinerant lifestyle he and his family might have endured had timing and fortune not been with him.

"If Chuck never would have called I would have been bouncing all over the country," Hoak said.

REMEMBERING "MOE"

Maurice "Moe" Matthews was not known by most Steelers fans but his sudden passing on March, 22, 2015, at the age of 53, hit folks within the organization hard. Matthews was a fixture at the team's practice facility and not just because he had been a chef in the cafeteria for years.

Morris served up as many laughs as he did food and he always seemed to have a smile and a quip for anyone that passed through the serving line. His popularity was such who former Steelers defensive backs coach Ray Horton set an unofficial record for most lopsided car sales ever.

Horton, before leaving for a job as defensive coordinator of the Cardinals in 2011, asked Matthews how much money he had in his pocket.

Matthews produced $20 and Horton tossed him the keys to a 1999 Mercedes-Benz SL. "Moe" smiled easily but especially so when you asked him about the red sports car he cared for like a baby.

Instead, he never had to stray far from his native Jeannette, which is about 20 miles east of Pittsburgh.

Hoak became a fixture on the Steelers' staffs and coached for Noll from 1971 to 1991 and Bill Cowher from 1992 to 2006.

He coached a Who's Who of Steelers running backs, from Franco Harris and Rocky Bleier to Jerome Bettis and Willie Parker.

"Dick Hoak was amazing to me. He allowed me to go out and flourish and do what I do with minimal interruption," said Bettis, a 2015 inductee into the Pro Football Hall of Fame. "He coached the play, not the actual players. He never once said, 'You've got to go here.' He said,

Franco Harris, shown with the "Italian Army" early in his career, is among a handful of standout running backs that Dick Hoak mentored during a coaching career that is the longest in Steelers' history.

'This is how the play is supposed to run and you go out and do what God has blessed you to do.' He said that's the way he's always taught and it's been very effective."

Hoak honed that approach as a young coach, and his acumen didn't just earn him the respect of the Steelers' running backs over the years.

"I've been with some coaches that have been around as long as him and they're stuck in their ways a little bit and he was never like that," former Steelers guard Alan Faneca said. "He was always coming up with new ideas, new schemes and had great ways to blend in some things he had seen a long time ago. I think he always used to say, 'We used to do this 20 years ago and then everybody forgot about it and now we're all doing it again.'"

Hoak's reputation spread beyond the Steelers, and twice he turned down a chance to become the head coach of the United States Football League's Pittsburgh Maulers. He also passed when Tony Dungy offered him a job of offensive coordinator after Dungy became head coach of the Tampa Bay Buccaneers in 1996.

His loyalty to the Rooneys and Steelers never allowed Hoak to seriously entertain other offers. He never forgot how Art Rooney twice gave him bonuses he never expected during the 1968 season, one in which Hoak made the Pro Bowl. Or how Art Rooney visited him every morning in 1970 when Hoak spent almost a week in the hospital after sustaining a concussion and dealing with complications from several broken blood vessels.

Hoak gave serious thought to riding out in retirement with Bettis after the Steelers won the 2005 Super Bowl. He returned for one more season to see if the Steelers could defend their title, something they didn't get a chance to do after going 8–8 and missing the playoffs.

Hoak's place in Steelers history is secure, and in a measure of how much he meant to the organization the team held a news conference

Miller ranked second in team history in catches (592) and fourth in receiving yards (6,569) and touchdown receptions (45) when he walked away from the game.

Miller will never go down as one of the flashy draft picks in Steelers history—they took him in the first round in 2005 and 30th overall—but he is one of their better ones. The 2005 tight end crop was such a weak one that only nine players at that position were among the 255 drafted. Of those nine only three were taken in the first four rounds. And only one other tight end in that draft class—journeyman Alex Smith—enjoyed a lengthy NFL career like Miller.

The Steelers had the luxury of building around Miller at tight end for more than a decade, and the two-time Super Bowl winner will go down as one of the most appreciated players within the organization and one of the most underrated players outside of it.

Not a bad legacy, and a perfect one for the understated Miller.

Had a camera been on him for any of the tributes that followed his retirement he would have blushed, but in a chapter with an appreciation theme it made perfect sense to celebrate Miller and his career yet again. His remarkably consistent approach to everything—whether it was playing, practicing or, heck, probably taking out the garbage—made him someone to emulate.

And that is in the Steelers' locker room and outside of it.

A Hard Goodbye for a Franchise Great

Alan Faneca woke up on February 6, 2006, and simply screamed. Images of winning the Super Bowl—and celebrating with his teammates as confetti fluttered in the charged air—hadn't been any more dormant than Faneca, and the perennial Pro Bowl guard didn't try to contain his emotions after less than an hour of sleep.

A little less than two years later, Faneca couldn't contain different emotions. The Steelers had just fallen to the Jacksonville Jaguars in an AFC playoff game, and Faneca sat in front of his locker at Heinz Field shortly after the 31–29 loss that ended Mike Tomlin's first season as the Steelers' head coach and bawled.

"I knew it was over and I just didn't want to let go," Faneca said.

Indeed, Faneca signed with the Jets two months later as an unrestricted free agent and played four more seasons, his final one with the Cardinals, before retiring.

His career, as decorated as it was, is a reminder that most players, even at the highest level of the game, don't get to script their finish. Jerome Bettis winning an elusive Super Bowl title—and in his hometown of Detroit—and then retiring is the rare instance of a player going out on top and leaving the game when he wants.

Faneca joined Franco Harris and Rod Woodson as all-time greats who left Pittsburgh because of differences over money. He still serves as a poignant reminder that the Steelers and the NFL are a business—and that the bottom line leads to unfortunate endings even for exalted players like Faneca, one of the five best offensive linemen in team history.

"It hurt to leave," Faneca said, "and when I look back on it now I think it was the perfect storm of everything wrong that could happen for someone going into a contract year and it just happened to land on my contract year."

Did it ever.

Bill Cowher retired after the 2006 season, taking with him the clout that could have been used to push for a new long-term contract for Faneca. In addition, the market for top-tier guards spiked, putting the Steelers in a position of committing big bucks to a player who would be entering his 10th NFL season.

An inevitable impasse turned acrimonious in April of 2007 when Faneca blasted Steelers management on the first day of mandatory minicamp and said the upcoming season would be his final one in Pittsburgh. Faneca did not let a strained relationship with management affect his play as he again anchored an offensive line that helped Willie Parker lead the NFL in rushing before the speedy running back broke his leg in the penultimate game of the season.

Faneca earned first-team All-Pro honors, cementing his status as one of the premier guards of his generation. He signed a five-year, $40 million contract with the Jets and made two more Pro Bowls in New York.

Faneca said he and the Steelers never came close to a new deal even though the Steelers reportedly made a push to re-sign him before the start of free agency. He said he wishes he could have played his entire career in Pittsburgh and a strong argument can be made that the Steelers erred by not signing Faneca to a long-term contract in 2007 given the state of their offensive line.

"It is a regret," Faneca said of playing elsewhere, "but there aren't many guys that get to stay for 10 years in one place and not many guys get to finish in one place for sure."

Faneca has made peace with how his time in Pittsburgh ended and he still stays in touch with many of his former Steelers teammates. He did not return to Pittsburgh for a 10th anniversary celebration of the 2005 Super Bowl championship team in 2015 but not because of any animosity toward the organization.

The weekend of the reunion Faneca and his wife, Julie, had to attend a funeral in New York. They planned to drive to Pittsburgh for the Steelers' November 15 game against the Browns but they couldn't travel because of a sick child.

"I really wish I would have been able to get back for the anniversary," Faneca said, "but Jerome's [Pro Football Hall of Fame] induction was like a reunion too and that was great seeing so many guys I hadn't seen in five or 10 years."

. . . .

Two More Reluctant Exits

Hines Ward and Troy Polamalu are two all-time greats who retired as Steelers though not necessarily on their own terms.

The Steelers released Ward in 2012 and he pondered playing elsewhere before officially announcing his retirement during a tearful news conference. The Steelers quietly pushed for Polamalu to retire after the 2014 season in which he didn't record a sack or an interception for only the second time in his career.

Polamalu, wanting little fanfare as possible, called Dan Rooney in April and then called longtime Steelers beat writer Jim Wexell to announce his retirement. He quietly slipped off the radar but stayed true to himself until the very end.

Polamalu played with the reckless abandon and choreographed chaos—even in his 12th and final NFL season—that made him one of the best safeties of his generation. His style, and the injuries that resulted from it, eventually robbed him of his legs.

Polamalu left the game as arguably the most unique Steelers star of all time.

He didn't like drawing attention to himself yet his play made it impossible to take your eyes off him. His long, flowing hair made him an ideal spokesman for Head & Shoulders and Polamalu seemed natural as a pitch man. Yet his aversion to self-promotion was such that when Polamalu visited sick kids at Children's Hospital of Pittsburgh he slipped in and out of the building so no one would notice him.

I never could reconcile how a man so soft-spoken and humble off the field could be so hard-hitting and intense on it. Polamalu is a deeply religious and spiritual person so I asked Father Paul Taylor at St. Vincent College if he could explain it.

Taylor, a Benedictine monk, works closely with the Steelers during training camp and also leads a mass before games at Heinz Field. He said the dichotomy of Polamalu made perfect sense.

"One of Troy's many gifts is that he has the gift of 100 percent focus. When he's praying, he's all in praying and when he's speaking with you, you're the only person in the room," Taylor said. "And when he was on the field he was 100 percent focused. He knew where every player was, he knew where the ball was and was able to respond to that with his whole being. Very few people, I think, have the gift of 100 percent focus. I have never seen Troy distracted because when he's doing something he's all in."

Concussions and the Complicated Legacy of Mike Webster

T he Steelers' annals are overflowing with tough guys who handled themselves on the field and played through all kinds of injuries. Mike Webster has one thing on all of them: nobody played more games for the Steelers than Webster, and he was literally at the center of the collisions precipitated by every snap of the ball.

The brawny Webster played 220 games in 15 seasons for the Steelers. He redefined excellence at his position while winning four Super Bowls.

A conversation of the greatest centers in NFL history has to start with Webster. Sadly, a conversation on the potential price of glory in the NFL might also start with Webster. That is because "Iron Mike" died in 2002 at the age of 50 both a broke and broken man.

His mental health rapidly deteriorated after Webster retired from the NFL following the 1990 season and he spent stretches of the final years of his life homeless or living with his teenage son, Garrett. A study of Webster's brain following his death eventually led Dr. Bennet Omalu to establish a link between repeated head hits in football and dementia and other mental illnesses later in life.

Webster is the first former NFL player that Omalu diagnosed with chronic traumatic encephalopathy (CTE). The need for more research on brain trauma has only grown since then due to the premature deaths of more than a score of former NFL players, including Pro Football Hall of Fame linebacker Junior Seau, who committed suicide in 2012 at the age of 43.

The NFL has been portrayed as both dismissive and reactionary to the issue of concussions. Accusations and litigation have been leveled at the billion-dollar league, leaving people like Garrett Webster with mixed feelings about the NFL.

Webster, who was forced to take care of his dad when it should have been the other way around, is the only one of his four siblings who still lives in the Pittsburgh area. He manages an airport parking service in Robinson Township and works as an administrator for the National Brain Institute.

The group, led by Omalu and Dr. Julian Bailes, is among the institutions that study brains to gain more clarity between repeated head hits and mental illnesses later in life.

"I think the biggest misconception is that groups like us are out to end football or stop people from playing football. Really what we're trying to do is make it safer," said Garrett Webster, who is in his early thirties. "There's no reason not to make the game safer and the NFL continuously tries to push the problem over here or push it over there."

The Webster family is upset that the NFL and the Steelers did not do more to take care of Mike Webster after his health collapsed and a series of bad investments wiped him out financially. The NFL fought a lawsuit by Webster's estate seeking disability payments and Garrett Webster said the family has only been invited to a pair of Steelers functions since his father's death.

When asked if his family has hard feelings toward the Steelers, Garrett Webster said, "Me and my mom will say this: we root for the players, we root for the jerseys. The suits or whatever you want to call them, those are the people we don't root for because all of this stuff didn't need to be this way. As a family we've been through so much since Dad retired it's continuously baffling to us why they don't want to make any kind of amends and not even amends, just some kind of acknowledgment. It seems like '[Bleep] the Websters' every time something comes up and that's disappointing. If they would have just embraced us and said, 'Hey, we're going to do what we can' and make us feel welcome and come in for alumni games one time a year or one time every two years that would have felt good at least. But instead it's, 'Nope, we're just going to ignore you guys,' and that just hurts."

That feeling of isolation characterized the final years of Mike Webster.

"My dad never complained that he played football," Garrett Webster said. "He was upset that he did all of this stuff and was part of the league and part of a team but once you can't do anything for them anymore you're a pariah. We're not mad at football. My dad won four Super Bowls, he made lifelong friends. [But] a lot of people should know, 'Hey, as of right now, if this stuff happens to you guess what? You're screwed.' That's what our argument has been with the NFL, is that this stuff happened and when you guys knew about it instead of doing the right thing, saying, 'Hey Mike, let's get you in. Let's study this while you're alive,' they just ignore him and pretend it doesn't exist."

Webster is not the only former Steelers offensive lineman whose erratic behavior and premature death was linked to head trauma as a result of football.

Former Steelers guard Terry Long committed suicide in 2005 at the age of 45. Former Steelers tackle Justin Strzelczyk died instantly a year earlier after the pickup truck he was driving rammed into a tanker during a high-speed police chase.

Omalu diagnosed Strzelczyk, who played nine seasons for the Steelers and left behind a wife and two young children, with CTE following an extensive study of his brain.

Strzelczyk's behavior after he retired from the NFL had led his wife, Keana McMahon, to divorce him because she didn't understand it and feared what he might do. More than a decade after Strzelcyk's death she refuses to watch an NFL game even though she still lives in the Pittsburgh area.

"NFL Sunday doesn't exist for me anymore," McMahon told the *Pittsburgh Tribune-Review* in December of 2015. "They don't care. The

Big Ben Advances Concussion Transparency

A breakthrough on concussions might have occurred when Ben Roethlisberger told doctors he was experiencing difficulty with his peripheral vision after taking a shot to the head in a November 29, 2015 game at Seattle.

The symptoms prompted the Steelers to pull Roethlisberger from the game and he was lauded for reporting them rather than trying to playing through a concussion in a close game.

Roethlisberger admitted that he might not have reported his symptoms early in his career without the benefit of foresight—and stature.

"You don't want to think about after football with your head, but you have to," Roethlisberger told reporters three days after the Seattle game. "You have to think about the type of man, husband, and father you want to be when you are done playing, because this is such a short part of our lives."

players are cattle to them. They're in and they're out and I won't watch it."

The link between football and brain injuries, however, is as complicated an issue as it is a contentious one.

Brains cannot be studied for CTE until after a person's death. And right now it is impossible to know which players are more prone to the degenerative brain disease until it is too late since only a fraction of people who played in the NFL have been diagnosed with CTE.

There is anything but a consensus in the medical field when it comes to brain injuries and even Omalu and Bailes disagree on a key point.

Omalu, in an opinion piece for the *New York Times* in late 2015, wrote that children should not be allowed to play football. Bailes said he would merely advise parents to wait until their child is older before permitting them to play organized football.

Coverage of the differing opinions at least showed that awareness on potential long-term repercussions from repeated hits to the head has spread. That, Garrett Webster said, is as much a priority for the

National Brain Institute as research on the body's most mysterious organ.

Alan Faneca is among former and current NFL players who take the issue seriously.

Faneca said he retired after 13 NFL seasons even though the Arizona Cardinals wanted him to return in 2011 because he wanted to play it safe with his long-term health.

Faneca, who has three young children, said he thinks about the potential fallout from all of the collisions he endured in football and has been proactive in dealing with it. Faneca runs regularly and takes supplements. He also engages in brain LaMantia, which is a series of exercises that work out the brain.

"Just keeping it active and doing things," Faneca said. "Not just sitting around doing nothing. Use it or lose it."

This approach coupled with medical breakthroughs could help generations of former NFL players navigate life after football. Greater awareness could also prompt former players to seek assistance when dealing with CTE.

Webster's youngest son acknowledges that pride often kept his father from accepting help from the Steelers and former teammates because he didn't want to take what he saw as charity.

Former Steelers running back Frenchy Fuqua saw a glimpse of Webster's plight near the end of Webster's life. The two were among a handful of Steelers players who attended an autograph show in Chantilly, Virginia, in 2002.

They were catching up on old times at the hotel bar and Fuqua noticed that Webster took a long time to speak before answering a question and seemed forgetful. What really struck Fuqua is when Webster told him he was sleeping in his car that night so he could pocket the money the former players had been given to stay in the hotel.

Fuqua said he tried to talk Webster into staying in his room—and accepting more than the $50 Fuqua insisted he take—but Webster refused.

"He was very proud and I can understand the pride that's involved to be in that situation but I had no idea it was that bad," said Fuqua, who held Webster in the highest regard as a person and a player. "He spent the night in his car and the next thing I know they were rushing him back to a hospital in Pittsburgh."

Webster died at the age of 50 and the cause of death has never been released by his family. What is particularly heart-wrenching about Webster's story is that even after his life unraveled he still felt a connection to the Steelers—as ambivalent as it was.

"Even in the end when my dad would say he couldn't stand the Steelers and Dan Rooney and stuff like that, we'd sit there and the Steelers would be on TV because it's Pittsburgh," Garrett Webster said. "Dad would still kind of pay attention to the game and you could tell he was still into it and wanted to root for the Steelers but it was like he felt guilty. We as a family were like that too. We always secretly wanted them to win."

· ·

Deaths of Former Teammates Hit Home for Webster Successor

Dermontti Dawson did not know much about the Steelers when they took him in the second round of the 1988 NFL draft. He had followed Miami more than any other NFL team because his quickness and strength had drawn comparisons to Dolphins center Dwight Stephenson. Dawson even wore No. 57 as a guard at Kentucky because of Stephenson, though he started emulating another all-time great center shortly after he arrived in Pittsburgh.

Webster was nearing the end of his storied career with the Steelers by the time Dawson joined the team. He was a big reason why Dawson was ready when the latter became a starter at guard in the fourth game of his rookie season—and the next season when Dawson took over at center for Webster.

"He was in there early looking at film, getting his weights out of the way. He was first in line of every drill, I don't care how hot," Dawson recalled of Webster. "I saw the way he prepared and took notes throughout the course of the season even though he knew the offense probably as well as the offensive coordinator, Tom Moore. I would always ask, 'Mike, why are you taking so many notes?' He said, 'Well, I just want it ingrained in my brain so it becomes second nature.' I started to do the same thing and I took as many notes as I could. Anything the coach would emphasize I was writing it down. I give a lot of praise to Mike for my success. He was a consummate pro and that's what he taught me."

Dawson more than upheld the Steelers' legacy at center, and in 2012 he joined his former mentor in the Pro Football Hall of Fame. By then Webster had been gone for a decade but the tragic end to his life led to Omalu's groundbreaking diagnosis of CTE and kept Webster at the forefront of the concussion issue.

Webster's story made the link between concussions and mental illness later in life more personal to Dawson. So did the fact that he had also been teammates with Long and Strzelcyzk.

Dawson wouldn't be human, given such context, if he didn't worry about suffering serious consequences from an NFL career that spanned 13 seasons and included a streak of 170 consecutive games played, third-most in Steelers history.

"I'm 50 years old and I know I have some short-term memory issues but I still try to play crossword puzzles and do things to offset them," Dawson said in January 2016. "I play brain games, I read newspapers, magazines, books. I'm always doing something cognitively and also a big thing for me is just getting outside to walk."

At least one former Steelers player is already experiencing trouble with walking, and Antwaan Randle-El entered the NFL two seasons after Dawson retired.

Randle-El told the *Pittsburgh Post-Gazette* in January 2016 that he has trouble making it up and down stairs because of the physical abuse from football and that he is already having issues with memory loss.

Randle-El said he would pursue a career in baseball if he had to do it over again and his admission came when *Concussion*, the story of Omalu's CTE breakthrough and his fight to be heard by the NFL, was still playing in movie theaters around the country.

The two shined an uncomfortable light on football and reinforced that the specter of concussions hangs over the NFL even while it is as popular and lucrative as ever.

Players, former and current ones, seem more willing to talk about the long-term danger of repeated concussions—or at least acknowledge it—and Dawson said that is a positive step toward changing the culture of the sport, though only a step.

"They've got new programs and protocol in place but unless a player decides to tell someone what's going on in his life and what struggles he's having it's not going to do any good," Dawson said. "I think we just have to keep preaching to the guys that pride comes before the fall. We've got to quit being so prideful and hiding things, especially when it comes to your mental and physical health. People can't help you unless you tell them what's going on."

Chapter 7

Putting the Steelers' Past into a Fun Perspective and Looking Ahead

rush for 1,316 yards in 15 games, despite hard feelings over not getting the kind of long-term contract offer Faneca believed the organization had promised him. Faneca made two more Pro Bowls while with the New York Jets and the 1998 first-round draft pick made the NFL's All-Decade team for the 2000s.

G: Sam Davis—He probably doesn't get his due as one of the Steelers' undrafted success stories. Davis made the Steelers in 1967, prior to coach Chuck Noll's arrival, and started at left guard from 1970 to '79. Davis neutralized Pro Football Hall of Famer Randy White in two Super Bowl wins over the Dallas Cowboys and the Steelers' backs loved running behind him because of his rapport with them and ability to make in-game adjustments.

C: Mike Webster—The Steelers have an impressive lineage at center from Chuck Cherundolo and Ray Mansfield to Dermontti Dawson, Jeff Hartings, and Maurkice Pouncey. None stands out more than "Iron Mike." Webster made nine Pro Bowls and earned seven first-team All-Pro selections while anchoring the offensive line that helped the Steelers win four Super Bowls in the 1970s.

OT: Larry Brown—The four-time Super Bowl winner crafted one of the more unique careers in Steelers history. Brown played tight end for six seasons and caught the Steelers' first touchdown pass in Super Bowl history. He moved to right tackle and became a mainstay there for eight seasons. Brown made the Pro Bowl in 1982 and played so well as an offensive lineman that Chuck Noll believed he merits a spot in the Pro Football Hall of Fame. That's good enough for me.

DL: Joe Greene—"Mean Joe" made the Pro Bowl 10 times, the only player in franchise history to accomplish that feat, and twice won NFL Defensive Player of the Year honors. The Steelers credit him with 66 career sacks, fourth-most in franchise history, even though it did not become an official NFL statistic until after Greene retired.

DL: Ernie Stautner—One of the toughest players in franchise history was also the lone player to have his jersey retired by the Steelers until Greene joined him in that honor in 2014. Stautner missed just six games in his 14-year career, playing through numerous injuries, and he made nine Pro Bowls and won the NFL's Best Lineman Award in 1957.

DL: L.C. Greenwood—Greenwood tormented opposing quarterbacks after Pittsburgh unearthed the defensive end in the 10th round of the 1969 draft—234 picks after it selected Greene. Greenwood is third on the Steelers' all-time sacks list (73.5) and made six Pro Bowls. It is a football injustice that Greenwood, who passed away at the age of 67, is not in the Pro Football Hall of Fame.

DL: Casey Hampton—The Steelers simply didn't allow teams to run the ball with Hampton at nose tackle. They allowed just 86.5 rushing yards per game from 2001 to '12, and Hampton made five Pro Bowls during that span. The Steelers' defense was predicated on stopping the run and forcing opponents into obvious passing situations. That all started with Hampton on the defenses that led the Steelers to three Super Bowls and two world titles from 2005 to '10.

LB: Jack Ham—No less an authority than Dan Rooney considers Ham one of the greatest linebackers of all time. His combination of brains and brawn allowed Ham to make eight consecutive Pro Bowls and his 32 career interceptions still rank seventh on the team's all-time list. Ham made a critical pick in the 1974 AFC Championship Game, sending the Steelers to their first Super Bowl.

LB: Jack Lambert—The two-time NFL Defensive Player of the Year delivered nasty hits even when he wasn't owning the middle of the field as Dallas safety Cliff Harris found out in the 1978 Super Bowl. Lambert body-slammed Harris for taunting Roy Gerela after a missed field goal and he was more than just an enforcer; he led the Steelers in tackles for 10 consecutive seasons. Lambert also made 28 career interceptions, which is still good for 10th on the Steelers' all-time list.

LB: James Harrison—The most unlikely Steelers success story this side of Rocky Bleier. Harrison made the most of his fourth chance with the Steelers and after playing behind Joey Porter for three seasons he blossomed into one of the most dominant pass rushers in the NFL. Harrison is second on the Steelers' all-time sacks list (74.5) and he put an exclamation point on his 2008 season, when he won NFL Defensive Player of the Year honors, with his 100-yard interception return for a touchdown in the Super Bowl.

LB: Andy Russell—Russell, one of the few players who survived a purge that Chuck Noll started after becoming the Steelers' head coach in 1969, wins this spot over a host of worthy candidates, including Greg Lloyd, Levon Kirkland, Jason Gildon, Joey Porter, and James Farrior. Russell made seven Pro Bowls and helped anchor the defense on the Steelers' first two Super Bowl–winning teams. Russell intercepted 18 passes during his career and he returned a pick 93 yards for a touchdown in a 1975 playoff win over the Baltimore Colts.

CB: Mel Blount—Wide receivers who thrive in today's pass-happy NFL should send Blount a thank-you card. He so physically dominated receivers during a Hall-of-Fame career that the NFL changed the rules to limit the contact defensive players could make with receivers. Blount, a four-time first-team All-Pro selection and the NFL's Defensive Player of the Year in 1975, leads the Steelers with 57 career interceptions. He is tied for 13th on the NFL's all-time list.

CB: Rod Woodson—It is tough to leave Jack Butler, another Pro Football Hall of Famer, off this team, but Woodson was one of the most dynamic players of his generation and a member of the NFL's 75th Anniversary All-Time Team. Woodson returned five interceptions, two kickoffs, and two punts for touchdowns and the former first-round draft pick made the Pro Bowl in seven of his 10 seasons with the Steelers. Woodson is fourth on the Steelers with 38 career interceptions and his 4,894 kickoff return yards are first on the team's all-time list.

S: Donnie Shell—The hard-hitting safety is another one of the Steelers' great success stories. Shell made the team in 1974 as an undrafted free agent out of South Carolina State and he consistently walloped players who managed to get past the Steelers' front seven. He could also cover as evidenced by Shell's 51 career interceptions, which put him behind only Blount and Butler, on the Steelers' all-time list.

S: Troy Polamalu—One of the most popular Steelers of all time, Polamalu played all over the field and made it impossible to scheme for the eight-time Pro Bowler. Polamalu had a flair for making highlight-reel plays, and his interception return for a touchdown in the 2008 AFC Championship Game might be at the top of that list. Polamalu is tied for seventh on the Steelers' all-time list with 32 interceptions.

K: Gary Anderson—His 1,343 career points lead the Steelers and may never be eclipsed. Anderson, who played for the Steelers from 1982 to '94, converted 78.2 percent of his field-goal attempts and made eight field goals from at least 50 yards. He and Kris Brown share the team record for the longest field goal (55 yards).

P: Bobby Walden—A member of the Steelers' first two Super Bowl Championship teams, Walden still leads the franchise for career punts (716). Walden punted for the Steelers from 1968 to 1977 and his 45.2 yards per punt in 1970 is still tied for fifth in Steelers history for punting average in a season.

. . . .

Steelers Mount Rushmore(s)

For someone who has never actually seen Mount Rushmore, I sure spend a lot of time debating Mount Rushmores for various sports teams and popular culture.

Picking a Mount Rushmore for the Steelers is especially difficult because there are so many worthy candidates for so few spots. I wimped out, to a degree, as I picked Mount Rushmores for players through the 1970s and players after the '70s, as well as one for coaches and front-office people. I also picked an ultimate Steelers Mount Rushmore, four towering figures in an organization that produced an abundance of them and added a fun/miscellaneous Mount Rushmore. Even with all of these I agonized over some of the picks and who I had to leave off the lists.

Players Through the 1970s: DT Joe Greene, DT Ernie Stautner, RB Franco Harris, and LB Jack Lambert.

How could I leave Terry Bradshaw off the list? Good question, and the only answer I have is that I also had to leave Mike Webster, Mel Blount, John Stallworth, and Jack Ham, among others, off the list. Greene, the best player in franchise history, is a no-brainer. So is Stautner, the first player to have his number retired by the Steelers. Harris conjures images of "Franco's Italian Army" and the "Immaculate Reception" but he also is the Steelers' and Super Bowl's most productive rusher. Lambert's gap-toothed scowl is the picture of the Steelers in the 1970s when they muscled their way into the NFL's elite franchises.

Players After the 1970s: WR Hines Ward, RB Jerome Bettis, S Troy Polamalu, and QB Ben Roethlisberger.

There are some cringe-worthy omissions, from Rod Woodson and Jason Gildon to Joey Porter and James Harrison but, again, there are only four spots. Ward ran away with all of the Steelers' major receiving records and also blocked with such ferocity that his fingerprints are on NFL rules that protect defenseless players. Bettis is the Steelers' second-leading rusher and one of their great all-time leaders. His punishing running style meshed perfectly with Pittsburgh's blue-collar sensibilities. Polamalu became a Steelers icon in large part because you simply could not take your eyes off him—whether you were an opposing quarterback or a fan watching from the comfort of a couch. He and Ed Reed are the best safeties of their generation. The Steelers had a lot of good teams after the '70s, but it took the drafting of Roethlisberger and his rapid rise for the Steelers to finally add one for the thumb. Roethlisberger is the biggest reason why the Steelers haven't had a losing record since 2003 and played in three Super Bowls since 2005.

Non-Players: Art Rooney, Chuck Noll, Dan Rooney, and Bill Nunn.

Art Rooney might have been the patriarch of the Steelers but he carried himself with a common touch that still permeates the organization. The Steelers' founder was beloved by his players and the city of Pittsburgh. Noll is the only coach to win four Super Bowls without losing in the big game. He changed the Steelers' culture as soon as he arrived in Pittsburgh as a 38-year-old first-time head coach. Dan Rooney came into his own as an executive after Noll's arrival and the two embraced the philosophy of building through the draft. He also emerged as one of driving forces behind policies, such as shared TV revenue, that allowed the NFL to thrive and become a billion-dollar industry. And the aptly named "Rooney Rule" has created more opportunities for minorities in coaching and the front office because of Dan Rooney. Nunn, a newspaperman turned scout, helped establish a Steelers pipeline to historically black colleges whose players were often overlooked. His work helped change the culture in the NFL and there should be a place in the Pro Football Hall of Fame for Nunn. It's hard to leave Art Rooney Jr., the architect of the drafts that turned the Steelers into a dynasty, off this list and you could make a strong case for him.

Steelers' Ultimate Mount Rushmore: Art Rooney, Joe Greene, Chuck Noll, and Dan Rooney.

Man, it's hard to have only one player among this foursome considering all of the great ones the Steelers have had. But Greene is clearly the best player in franchise history and the other three are towering figures in the organization and the NFL in general.

"Mean" Joe Greene (75) runs with a fumble during a game against the Philadelphia Eagles in Pittsburgh, November 3, 1974. The Steelers defeated the Eagles 27-0 at Three Rivers Stadium. (AP Photo/NFL Photos)

Steelers' Miscellaneous Mount Rushmore: The Terrible Towel, Frenchy Fuqua's platform shoes and L.C. Greenwood's gold cleats, Bill Cowher's chin, and Brett Keisel's beard.

Nothing better symbolizes the Steelers' popularity beyond Western Pennsylvania than fans waving Terrible Towels at games away from Heinz Field. The 1970s Steelers were as colorful as they were talented. The preferred footwear by Fuqua and Greenwood were expressions of the former. Nothing said Pittsburgh more than Cowher's chin and jutted jaw and Keisel's beard took on a life of its own after he grew it out, inspiring Twitter accounts and an annual charity event that raises money for cancer research.

How Well Do You Know Your Steelers?

The Steelers lend themselves to trivia contests because of their rich history, and you can make them easy or harder than Cowher's chin.

I split the difference, though leaning toward the more difficult side, with a 20-question quiz that is a template for trivia tests.

Here is the grading scale for the test in which there are 36 possible points: 0–10 right and you are obviously a Ravens spy; 11–20 and you need to do more homework; 21–25 and you pass; 26–30 and you are hard-core about your Steelers; 31–36 and congratulations, you get to manage Mike Tomlin's timeouts and coaches' challenges for an entire season.

Here is the test:

1. I led the Steelers with six interceptions in 1978 and went undrafted after playing quarterback in college. I won a historic Super Bowl as a head coach and gave Mike Tomlin one of his early breaks. Who am I?

2. Ben Roethlisberger threw his 213th career touchdown pass in a 2013 game, passing Terry Bradshaw for the most in franchise history. Who caught that touchdown pass?

3. The Steelers inaugurated a team MVP award in 1969. Since then four different players have won it three times, including Antonio Brown, the 2015 recipient of the award. Who are the three others who have been three-time Steelers MVPs?

4. The Steelers have allowed five 200-yard rushing games in franchise history. One player has two of those games and he is in the Pro Football Hall of Fame. Name him.

5. Match the Steelers player with the correct alma mater: Antonio Brown, Merril Hoge, Eric Green and Mel Blount.

6. I led the NFL in rushing both of the two full seasons I played for the Steelers and I played for two other NFL teams. I was inducted into the Pro Football Hall of Fame in 1966. Who am I?

7. Four of the Steelers' first five picks in the historic 1974 NFL draft eventually made the Pro Football Hall of Fame. Name the player who didn't and the round he was drafted.

8. Troy Polamalu intercepted 32 passes during his career and had at least one pick against 17 different teams. A quarter of his interceptions, however, came against one team. Which team was that?

9. Two Steelers are tied for the longest service by a defensive player, 14 seasons. Who are those players?

10. Chuck Noll, Bill Cowher, and Mike Tomlin all won their head-coaching debuts. Name the team the Steelers beat for each of the three coaches' first games.

11. Who are the two Steelers tight ends to catch a touchdown pass in the Super Bowl?

12. Rocky Bleier wrote a book that was turned into a TV movie. Who played Bleier in the movie? a) Ted Danson, b) Robert Urich, c) Steve Guttenberg d) Burt Reynolds.

13. I lead the Steelers with 827 career yards on interception returns and I am a member of the Pro Football Hall of Fame. Who am I?

14. In 2014, after throwing for 360 yards in a 27–20 win at Atlanta, Ben Roethlisberger became one of just six quarterbacks in NFL history to beat at least 31 teams. Who are the other five quarterbacks?

15. Which defensive player was voted Steelers MVP in 1974, the season the team broke through and won its first Super Bowl?

16. What quarterback did the Steelers select in the fifth round of the 2000 NFL draft, 36 picks before the New England Patriots took Tom Brady?

17. Quarterbacks rank first and second on the Steelers' all-time list for yards per carry players with a minimum of 1,500 rushing yards. Who are they?

18. What team has the Steelers beaten the most in the postseason?

19. The Steelers have won the Associated Press Defensive Player of the Year Award six times since it started in 1971, the most of any organization. Who was the only one of the six who never won a Super Bowl while playing for the Steelers?

20. Three coaches who are in the Pro Football Hall of Fame were among Chuck Noll's greatest influences. Name them.

Revisiting the Steelers' Drafts One More Time

Drafts are always fun to look back on because of the hits and misses and the what-ifs that accompany every selection process. The Steelers have enjoyed as much drafting success as any team since they made it a priority as far as team building in 1969.

Who are the best draft choices by round in team history? This is another subject that will generate robust debate, and here are mine for the first 10 rounds even though the draft once exceeded 20 rounds.

First Round: DT Joe Greene, 1969—So many candidates here from Terry Bradshaw, the first overall pick of the 1970 draft, to more recent selections such as Troy Polamalu (2003) and Ben Roethlisberger (2004). Still, the choice has to be Greene, who turned into the best player in franchise history.

Second Round: DT Ernie Stautner, 1950—How do you pass on Jack Lambert (1974) or Jack Ham (1972)? I'll let the two greats cancel out each other and go with Stautner, the first player in franchise history to have his number retired.

Third Round: CB Mel Blount, 1970—The Steelers found their all-time leading receiver (Hines Ward), their all-time sacks leader (Jason Gildon), and the fire and guts of their 2005 world championship team (Joey Porter) in the third round. They got a game-changer and a future Pro Football Hall of Famer in Blount, two rounds after landing Bradshaw.

Fourth Round: WR John Stallworth, 1974—Defensive ends Dwight White and Aaron Smith and cornerback Ike Taylor are among the players the Steelers drafted in this round. But Stallworth is the only Pro Football Hall of Famer they landed in the fourth round, and they got him in the same draft as Lynn Swann.

Fifth Round: C Mike Webster, 1974—Barry Foster, Hardy Nickerson, and Larry Brown were fifth-round picks but Mike Webster is one of the all-time great centers—and his career provided an exclamation point to the greatest draft in NFL history.

Sixth Round: WR Antonio Brown, 2010—Brown gets the nod over Greg Lloyd, the small-school find out of Fort Valley State who made five Pro Bowls for the Steelers and emerged as the face of "Blitzburgh." Brown leads the conversation for best wide receiver in the NFL right now, and six years into his career, the four-time Pro Bowler is blazing a path to Canton, Ohio.

Seventh Round: DE Brett Keisel, 2002—The 242nd overall pick of the 2002 draft developed into a cornerstone on the best Steelers defensive line since the famed "Steel Curtain." Running back Dick Hoak is a close second here given his contributions as a player—he was still sixth on the Steelers' all-time rushing list with 3,965 yards following the 2015 season—and then a coach.

Eighth Round: DT Ernie "Fats" Holmes, 1971—A member of the "Steel Curtain," Holmes is credited with 40 sacks in 82 career games. To put that number into perspective, consider that Greene is credited with 66 sacks in 181 games. Darren Perry, who is tied for seventh in Steelers history with 32 career interceptions, is also a consideration here.

Ninth Round: QB Johnny Unitas—What might have been had the Rooney sons, convinced that Unitas could play, sold their father on pulling rank on coach Walt Kiesling in 1955? Kiesling preferred veterans over rookies and refused to give Unitas a serious look in the latter's only training camp with the Steelers. The Steelers released him and the rest is history.

10th Round: DE L.C. Greenwood—Another member of the vaunted "Steel Curtain" that the Steelers found late in the draft. Put him in the Pro Football Hall of Fame already.

Notable: Linebacker Andy Russell and running back Rocky Bleier were 16th-round picks in 1963 and 1968, respectively. Elbie Nickel, the second-best tight end in Steelers history, was a 15th-round pick in 1947.

. . . .

Don't Forget About Free Agency

Free agency became a legitimate way for teams to reinforce their rosters in the early 1990s, but the Steelers are rarely if ever among the so-called winners in March.

The Steelers haven't ignored free agency; they have simply picked their spots while other franchises have habitually embarked on spending sprees that rarely transformed them into Super Bowl contenders.

Free-agent signings have loomed large in the Steelers returning to the Super Bowl four times and winning two of them since the 1970s. Here are the Steelers' top five free-agent signings:

LB James Farrior—The Steelers struck gold when they signed Farrior to a three-year, $5.125 million contract in 2002 after the New York Jets decided to part ways with their former first-round draft pick. Farrior made two Pro Bowls in 10 seasons with the Steelers and finished runner-up to Ed Reed for NFL Defensive Player of the Year honors in 2004. "Potsy," a name given to him by his mother because of his belly as a baby, stabilized the middle of the Steelers' defense and emerged as one of the best leaders in franchise history. Coach Mike Tomlin referred to him as the "alpha male" others rallied around in a locker room filled with strong personalities. No wonder Farrior's teammates voted him a captain for eight consecutive seasons.

S Ryan Clark—Clark overcame life-threatening complications from sickle-cell trait in 2007 to team with Troy Polamalu and give the Steelers their best safety tandem since Donnie Shell and Mike Wagner in the 1970s. Clark loved to talk, loved to hit, and he did a lot of both after signing a four-year, $7 million contract with the Steelers in 2007. The former undrafted free agent emerged as an ideal complement to Polamalu because the two close friends knew each other so well on and off the field. Clark was an underrated player on the 2008 defense that drove the Steelers' run to a record sixth Super Bowl title.

C Jeff Hartings—The Steelers signed the former Lions guard to a six-year, $24.75 million contract in 2001, and Hartings flourished in Pittsburgh despite changing positions and replacing future Pro Football Hall of Famer Dermontti Dawson. Hartings twice made the Pro Bowl and won a Super Bowl before retiring in 2007 because of recurring knee problems. He is part of the impressive lineage that the Steelers have at center.

OLB Kevin Greene—The newly minted Pro Football Hall of Famer played just three seasons in Pittsburgh after the Steelers signed him to a $5.35 million contract in 1993. But Greene and Greg Lloyd put the blitz in "Blitzburgh" and the former registered 35.5 sacks from 1993 to '95, including an NFL-best 14 in 1994. The Steelers played in the AFC Championship Game and the Super Bowl in Greene's final two seasons with the team and his time in Pittsburgh helped Greene make the All-NFL team in the 1990s.

RB DeAngelo Williams—The Carolina Panthers' all-time leading rusher signed a two-year, $4 million contract with the Steelers, and his addition proved to be crucial in 2015 after Le'Veon Bell played six games that were sandwiched between a suspension and a season-ending knee injury. Williams rushed for 907 yards and 11 touchdowns—the latter tied him for the most in the NFL—and he gave the Steelers a premium insurance policy a year after not having one may have cost the team a chance of making a run for the Super Bowl. Williams accepted his role as Bell's understudy when he signed with the Steelers and then did a pretty damn good impersonation of Bell while rejuvenating his career. A foot injury kept Williams out of the playoffs, and the Steelers might have made the Super Bowl had he not gotten hurt in their regular-season finale.

Steelers Takes from a Beat Writer

I was around the Steelers from 2006 to 2014 on a regular basis and so many things stand out from covering the team. Here are 10 of them in no particular order.

Surreal in the Super Bowl: Who knew a Cardinals team that went just 8–8 in the regular season would give the Steelers such a fight in Super Bowl XLIII? The Cardinals would have won if James Harrison didn't return an interception 100 yards for a touchdown at the end of the first half and Ben Roethlisberger didn't lead the finest fourth-quarter drive of his career after the Steelers' defense inexplicably faltered. Roethlisberger and Santonio Holmes hooked up for one of the greatest plays in Super Bowl history and Holmes' six-yard touchdown catch delivered a 27–23 win. And it was only the second-best play in that game.

Troy Polamalu's Touchdown in 2008 AFC Championship Game: The safety whose soft voice made him hard to hear in group interviews produced a roar for the ages with the play that secured the Steelers' spot in the Super Bowl. The Steelers were holding a tenuous

16–14 lead over the Ravens when Polamalu's pick-six sent fans into a frenzy. Even in the closed press box at Heinz Field it became ear-splittingly loud as Polamalu weaved his way to the end zone after intercepting rookie quarterback Joe Flacco. An exceptional moment delivered by an exceptional player.

Tim Tebow Throws Steelers for a Loop: The general feeling in the press box prior to a 2011 playoff game at Sports Authority Field at Mile High: no way would the Broncos beat the Steelers because their quarterback simply couldn't throw the ball with any consistency. All Tim Tebow did was pass for 316 yards—a number that had extra if not eerie significance given his strong religious convictions—against a defense that had led the NFL in passing defense in the regular season (171.9 passing yards allowed per game). Tebow passed for a grand total of 175 yards in non-preseason NFL games after that evisceration of the Steelers and he was soon out of the league.

Making a Statement for Dick LeBeau: Steelers defensive players wore LeBeau's No. 44 Lions jersey on multiple occasions to promote his candidacy for the Pro Football Hall of Fame. The gestures epitomized their love and respect for the longtime Steelers defensive coordinator. LeBeau's 62 career interceptions still rank 10th (tied) on the NFL's all-time list and he made all of those picks during a time when some coaches viewed the forward pass with as much suspicion as they did Communism. LeBeau should have been elected to the Pro Football Hall of Fame long before 2010, but when he finally got the call, coach Mike Tomlin made sure busloads of Steelers players were in Canton, Ohio, for his induction speech. The thing about LeBeau is he may be a better person than he was a player and coach.

Ben Roethlisberger's Redemption: Roethlisberger won two Super Bowls before he turned 27 but crashed hard in 2010 when he was accused of sexual assault for the second time in nine months. I give a ton of credit to Roethlisberger, who was never charged following either accusation, for turning his life around and becoming a worthy ambassador of the Steelers. And yes, he needed to make major changes but I always pose this question too: How would *you* handle the success and fame after becoming the youngest quarterback ever to win a Super Bowl? Covering Roethlisberger's fall from grace was exhausting and seemingly never-ending. But he worked hard to regain the trust of the organization and will go down as one of the most significant figures in franchise history.

The Steelers' Run to the Super Bowl in 2010: Few could have seen this coming in the wake of the Roethlisberger mess and his four-game suspension at the start of the season. Dennis Dixon, who would have entered the season at the No. 3 quarterback, started the first two games. Charlie Batch, who would have been the odd man out at quarterback if not for an injury suffered by backup Byron Leftwich at the end of the preseason, started the next two games. All the Steelers did was win three of those games. And only a late touchdown drive by the Ravens prevented the Steelers from winning all four games during Roethlisberger's suspension. The us-against-the-world mentality that coalesced in Pittsburgh's locker room became apparent after the Steelers trounced the Buccaneers 38–13 in Tampa. Coach Mike Tomlin took a defiant stance at his postgame news conference, saying that the Steelers hadn't listened to the naysayers or "elevator music" that preceded their 3–0 start.

From 0–4 to the Playoffs…Almost: The start of the 2013 season was an unmitigated disaster. The Steelers dropped their first four games and bottomed out with a London loss to the Vikings and journeyman quarterback Matt Cassel. Yet the Steelers would have made the playoffs had Ryan Succop not missed a 41-yard field goal in a Chiefs loss to the Chargers in one of the last games of the regular season. A Kansas City win was one of eight things that needed to happen for the Steelers to make the playoffs going into the penultimate week of the season. Seven of those things did happen… before the Chiefs lost in overtime. I will never forget those of us watching in disbelief in the Heinz Field press box as the Chiefs nearly beat the Chargers. The end produced a scene right out of Peanuts— Lucy pulling the ball away as Charlie Brown went to kick—leaving the Steelers to wonder what might have been had they not lost games to the Vikings and Raiders earlier in the season.

The Brilliance of Antonio Brown: One of the Steelers' off-season narratives for years? Their need to draft a tall wide receiver for quarterback Ben Roethlisberger. They found that transformative wideout late in the sixth round in 2010 in a player who is listed at 5'10" and 186 pounds. Brown plays much bigger than his size and his emergence pushed Hines Ward out of the starting lineup near the end of the 2011 season. The four-time Pro Bowler has put up staggering numbers—his 375 catches from 2013 to '15 are the most in NFL history during a three-season span—and helped change the perception that a wide receiver has to be a certain size to dominate a game. As easy as Brown makes it look while he routinely shreds opposing secondaries, he is not just a product of his immense physical gifts. Brown is a tireless worker, something that has elevated his game and those who are around him on a regular basis.

A Long Goodbye: A 2014 playoff loss to the Ravens produced a hushed Steelers locker room and a moment I can still see as if it happened yesterday. Brett Keisel was walking out of the locker room for the final time as a player when fellow defensive end Cameron Heyward grabbed him in a hug and didn't let go. Mentor and protégé spoke quietly as Heyward desperately tried to do the impossible and stop time. He didn't want Keisel to go any more than Steelers fans did, but everyone's time is up eventually. That scene offered a cruel, poignant reminder of that—and a metaphor for life in general.

An Unforgettable Experience: What started as a story about Steelers fan Heather Miller, who passed away in 2009 at the age of 11, turned into an unforgettable journey. Heather had formed a strong bond with Casey Hampton, Heath Miller, Troy Polamalu, and others in the Steelers organization during her fight against cancer and gave them as much as they gave her and her family. I wrote about that bond in 2010 and eventually Heather's mother, Wendy, and I wrote the book, *Heaven Sent: The Heather Miller Story.* Many things have stuck with me from that experience, including my belief that stories such as Heather's should be told at the NFL's annual rookie symposium. NFL players have the opportunity to make a difference in people's lives and it is something they should not take lightly.

What the Future Holds for the Steelers

One of Mike Tomlin's greatest strengths as a coach is not allowing any semblance of excuse to seep into the mindset of his players. Ask him about the impact of injuries and he will invariably cite them as being as much a part of football as blocking and tackling. Fittingly, the 2015 season affirmed that as cliché as the Steelers' "next man up" mantra is, few execute it better than they do.

The Steelers won 10 regular-season games despite a rash of injuries that forced them to start three different quarterbacks, plug in an untested NFL player at left tackle, and play all but six games without their All-Pro running back.

They won their first postseason game since the 2010 season at Cincinnati and nearly upset the Broncos in Denver in the divisional round of the playoffs. The Steelers played their final game without All-Pro wide receiver Antonio Brown and were down to undrafted free agent Fitzgerald Toussaint and journeyman Jordan Todman at running back because of injuries. Publicly Tomlin and the Steelers dismissed what might have been had they been healthier.

Privately the Steelers had to agonize over the missed opportunity to at least get back to the Super Bowl for the simple reason that quarterback Ben Roethlisberger turned 34 a month after the Broncos won it all in 2015.

The Steelers have said it is not time to start looking for Roethlisberger's eventual replacement in the NFL draft and he might well have another good five seasons left in him. But he is much closer to the end of what I believe is a Pro Football Hall of Fame career than the beginning of it.

What should make Steelers fans shudder is the number of quarterbacks the team went through between Terry Bradshaw and Roethlisberger. Instability at the position is the biggest reason why the Steelers made just one Super Bowl appearance from 1980 to 2004 and the position is both more important and harder to scout than ever with the proliferation of spread offenses at the college level.

The good news for the Steelers is they remain one of the most stable organizations in all of sports. They have a plan and are not prone to the kind of knee-jerk reactions that have some organizations in a perpetual chase of their tail. Tomlin and general manager Kevin Colbert work exceptionally well together, bound by mutual respect and a burning desire to win.

The Steelers have stood tall since Ben Roethlisberger burst onto the scene in 2004 as a rookie, winning a pair of Super Bowls. They have committed to maximizing his remaining seasons by surrounding Big Ben with elite talent.

Their relationship goes a long way toward heading off dysfunction and keeping everyone rowing, if you will, in the same direction. Neither is perfect, as some segment of Steelers fans expect them to be, but the Steelers have appeared in two Super Bowls, won one of them and have yet to post a losing season since Tomlin and Colbert have worked together.

Colbert said after the 2013 season that the Steelers planned to maximize Roethlisberger's remaining seasons and they have done that by surrounding him with talent. The offense alone, if it stays relatively healthy, should make the Steelers Super Bowl contenders for the foreseeable future. And a defense that the Steelers have rebuilt on the run will only get better with Keith Butler running it. Butler succeeded Dick LeBeau in 2015 and proved that he is more than capable as a defensive coordinator. Wait until he gets more pieces to bolster the Steelers' secondary and their pass rush.

It is impossible to predict when the Steelers will give headline writers everywhere a layup—Stairway to Seven, Seventh Heaven, Seven Up—by winning another Super Bowl. Their position of strength would quickly erode if Roethlisberger suffers a major injury—or the bill comes due for all the punishment he has absorbed in his first 12 NFL seasons.

One certain thing is that Terrible Towels will continue to wave in Heinz Field and stadiums across the country. There is too much of a foundation—from Art Rooney and Chuck Noll and the 1970s dynasty to the Steelers' run from 2005 to 2010—for fan support to fade.

Steelers' fans take as much pride in their fierce loyalty as they do their favorite team's success. That is why Steelers Nation is anything but a cliché—few organizations can actually make this claim—and it only seems to be growing. Hopefully members enjoyed this book and will use it as they cross off items on their Steelers bucket list.

Acknowledgments

This should be one of the easiest parts to write. The heavy lifting is finished and now it's a just a matter of thanking people. What makes it difficult is making sure I don't forget anyone who helped me during the reporting and writing of this book because there were so many.

First and foremost, I couldn't have done this without the support of my immediate family on many levels. One of the biggest thrills in doing this book was my dad accompanying me when I interviewed Al Vento, one of the founders of Franco's Italian Army, at his restaurant. My dad was as engrossed as I was listening to Al talk about "the Army," as he called it. An added bonus: my cousin Tom, who set up the interview, joined us and laughed along with us at the stories that truly came from a bygone era. Thanks to Al and his lunch group for welcoming us interlopers for a Saturday afternoon that we won't soon forget.

A special thanks to Dermontti Dawson for writing the foreword to the book and also conducting a lengthy interview for it. There isn't a nicer or classier guy than Dermontti.

A number of other Steelers, past and present, provided invaluable help. Some were more than generous with their time in giving insightful interviews. Others helped set up those interviews or provided background information. They include Charlie Batch, Jerome Bettis, Alan Faneca, Frenchy Fuqua, Jason Gildon, Joe Gordon, Dick Hoak, Michael Hustava, Tunch Ilkin, Brett Keisel, Burt Lauten, Bill Priatko, Tony Quatrini, Art Rooney Jr., Andy Russell, and John Simpson.

Buffalo Bills general manager and former Steelers director of pro personnel Doug Whaley was a great help, as was Steelers scout Mark Gorscak. I ran into "Gors" before the Steelers' 2015 regular-season finale and when I told him I was looking for a good tailgate he took me to the quintessential one. There I met people who have become friends through their love of the Steelers. They welcomed me as if I was one of their own and provided great color to the first chapter of the book. Those I interviewed include Bee

Huss, Bob and Dow Malnati, and Jennifer Piper. The group's only mistake: inviting me back, which it may come to regret.

Garrett Webster, the son of the late, great Mike Webster, was again more than gracious with his time and talking about a difficult subject. Father Paul Taylor and Oland "Dodo" Canterna and his wife, Shirley, were among those from St. Vincent College who sat down with me for the book. You can't talk about the Steelers without their connection to St. Vincent through training camp and Taylor and the Canternas were extremely helpful.

I did not want this book to simply be a recitation of the Steelers' history, as glorious as it is, or just from the perspective of former players, coaches, and others in the organization. To that end, I talked with fans, bar owners, and managers, heck even a former Cleveland Browns great. Thanks to Doug Dieken for giving me an interview, even after I told him I was calling about a Steelers book. Others I want to thank include Marty "Mop" Angiulli, Mark Beauregard, Dave Bryan (who owns the Steelers Depot website), Skip Brown, longtime Pittsburgh Post-Gazette beat writer Ed Bouchette, Mike Burrell, Tom Chaffee, Tom Diecks, Erin Fey, Jen Detore, Mary Jo Hartman, Jeremy Hill, Jason Hupp, Nikki Kemerer, Greg Morris, Tom Okon, Mark Schiller, Jeff Trebac, Hans "Walle" Walsten, Anne Williams, Tim Welty, and Don Zadach, who also answers to "Pope Yinzer."

I conducted almost 50 interviews for this book and would have loved to talk to 50 more people for it. But the deadline wasn't open-ended as much as I kept pushing for more time. I also drew on anecdotes and interviews from when I covered the team as well as interviews posted on the Steelers' website and nuggets gleaned from various news organizations, which I credited in the book. I am pleased with the end result and think there is something for every Steelers fan in this book since there are no shortage of bucket-list items when it comes to one of the greatest organizations in all of sports.

Thanks to Tom Bast of Triumph Books for the opportunity to execute the unique concept for this book and to editor Jesse Jordan for his skill and patience in guiding this project. If I left anyone out, I truly apologize.